Better Homes and Gardens®

Microwave Cooking for Kids

BETTER HOMES AND GARDENS® BOOKS
Editor: Gerald M. Knox
Art Director: Ernest Shelton
Managing Editor: David A. Kirchner

Food and Nutrition Editor: Nancy Byal
Department Head—Cook Books: Sharyl Heiken
Associate Department Heads: Sandra Granseth,
    Rosemary C. Hutchinson, Elizabeth Woolever
Senior Food Editors: Julie Henderson, Julia Malloy,
    Marcia Stanley
Associate Food Editors: Jill Burmeister,
    Molly Culbertson, Linda Foley, Linda Henry,
    Lynn Hoppe, Mary Jo Plutt, Maureen Powers,
    Joyce Trollope
Recipe Development Editor: Marion Viall
Test Kitchen Director: Sharon Stilwell
Test Kitchen Home Economists: Jean Brekke,
    Kay Cargill, Marilyn Cornelius, Maryellyn Krantz,
    Lynelle Munn, Dianna Nolin, Marge Steenson,
    Cynthia Volcko

Associate Art Directors: Linda Ford Vermie,
    Neoma Alt West, Randall Yontz
Copy and Production Editors: Marsha Jahns,
    Mary Helen Schiltz, Carl Voss, David A. Walsh
Assistant Art Directors: Harijs Priekulis, Tom Wegner
Senior Graphic Designers: Alisann Dixon,
    Lynda Haupert, Lyne Neymeyer
Graphic Designers: Mike Burns, Mike Eagleton,
    Deb Miner, Stan Sams, D. Greg Thompson,
    Darla Whipple, Paul Zimmerman

Vice President, Editorial Director: Doris Eby
Executive Director, Editorial Services: Duane L. Gregg

General Manager: Fred Stines
Director of Publishing: Robert B. Nelson
Vice President, Retail Marketing: Jamie Martin
Vice President, Direct Marketing: Arthur Heydendael

MICROWAVE COOKING FOR KIDS
Editors: Molly Culbertson, Julia Malloy
Copy and Production Editor: Marsha Jahns
Graphic Designer: Lyne Neymeyer
Electronic Text Processor: Donna Russell
Contributing Photographer: Mike Dieter
Contributing Illustrator: Thomas Rosborough

Our seal assures you that every
recipe in *Microwave Cooking for Kids*
has been tested by the Better Homes
and Gardens® Test Kitchen. This means
that each recipe is practical and
reliable, and meets our high standards
of taste appeal.

On the cover: *Super Sloppy Joe* (see recipe, page 38)

Contents

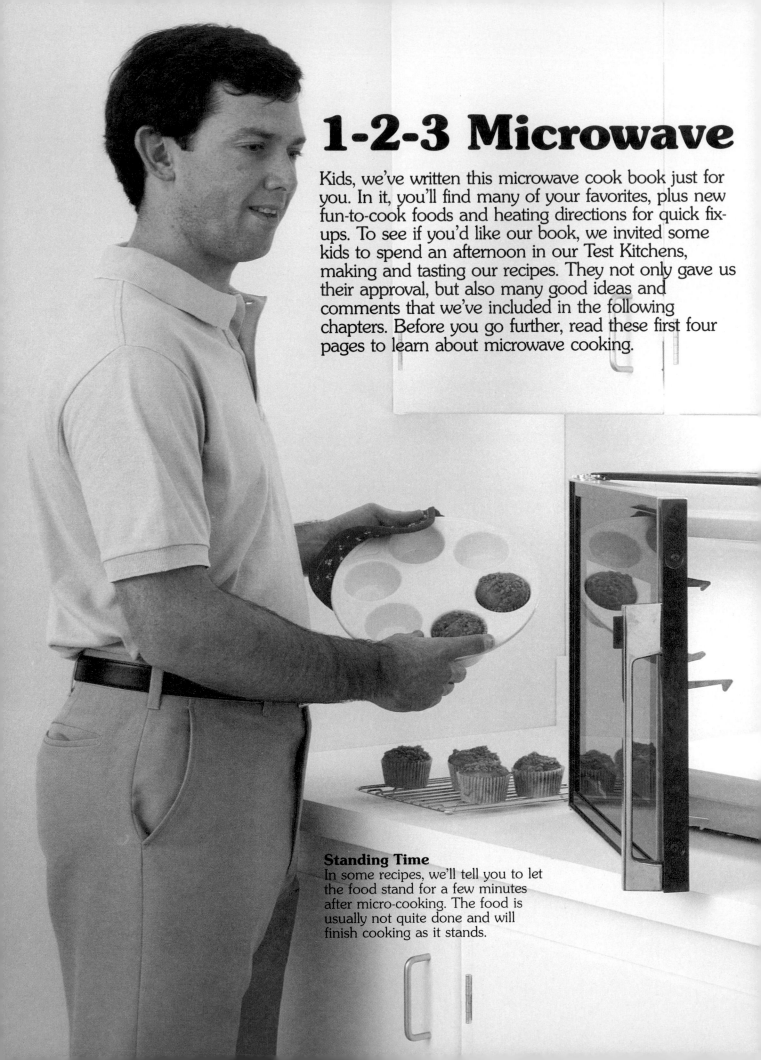

1-2-3 Microwave

Kids, we've written this microwave cook book just for you. In it, you'll find many of your favorites, plus new fun-to-cook foods and heating directions for quick fix-ups. To see if you'd like our book, we invited some kids to spend an afternoon in our Test Kitchens, making and tasting our recipes. They not only gave us their approval, but also many good ideas and comments that we've included in the following chapters. Before you go further, read these first four pages to learn about microwave cooking.

Standing Time
In some recipes, we'll tell you to let the food stand for a few minutes after micro-cooking. The food is usually not quite done and will finish cooking as it stands.

Your Microwave Oven

Microwave ovens are not all the same. Before you start micro-cooking, learn how to set your microwave oven on high and work the timer. Also, find out how many watts your oven has. We tested our recipes in 600- to 700-watt ovens. If yours has fewer watts, foods may take a little longer to cook.

Adult Helpers

Our recipes are easy enough to make by yourself, but have an adult close by for questions.

Microwave Cooking

Cooking in a microwave oven is almost always faster than regular cooking. It's so fast that sometimes you have to make sure that part of the food doesn't cook faster than the other parts and get overdone. We found that food cooks best and most evenly when it's in the center of the microwave oven. And for some recipes, stirring or moving a food around, or turning a dish, helps (we'll tell you when). You can often do this without even taking the dish from the oven.

Covering

In microwave cooking, covering a food makes it cook faster and more evenly, too. Whenever a dish is covered during cooking, remove the cover carefully, so the steam won't burn you. With adult help, use tongs or hot pads to lift the far side of the cover up first, letting the steam go out away from you.

Materials to Use

In micro-cooking, don't use metal saucepans. Use only nonmetal cookware or certain paper or plastic products. You can micro-cook on paper plates, towels, and napkins for up to 4 minutes. Just use white, not colored, paper products, because dyes come off.

Dishes to Use

Lots of nonmetal dishes you may already have in your kitchen work well in the microwave oven—heavy glass and ceramic casseroles, baking dishes, plates, measuring cups, and custard cups, to name a few. You also may have special microwave oven cookware. If you aren't sure whether a dish is microwave-safe, ask an adult.

Hot Pads for Hot Dishes

Keep hot pads nearby when you micro-cook, to use when you stir or uncover a food, or turn or take a dish from the oven. The heat of the food may make the dish too hot to handle with your hands.

Show and Tell

To be a good cook, you need to be organized before you start cooking. Follow these good habits every time, and you'll be on your way. First, wash and dry your hands. Then, gather all of the equipment and ingredients listed. Next, open any packages and cut or shred and measure ingredients, as necessary. We think the best way to explain cutting and measuring is to show you pictures and tell you what we mean.

Measuring Butter or Margarine

Use a table knife to cut a wrapped stick of butter or margarine at the mark you need, then unwrap it. One stick of butter or margarine equals one-half cup. The marks on the wrapper show the tablespoon, the one-fourth-cup, and often the one-third-cup measures.

Measuring Liquids

Put a glass or plastic measuring cup on a level surface and bend down so your eyes are even with the measurement mark you need. Carefully pour in the liquid till it reaches the mark. To measure a liquid in a measuring spoon, fill the spoon to the top.

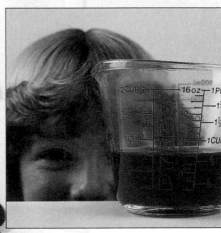

Draining Pasta and Vegetables

Put a colander into the sink. Ask an adult to help you carefully pour cooked pasta or vegetables out of the cooking dish into the colander. Pour slowly, because hot steam will rise out of the sink as you pour.

Greasing

Put a little butter or margarine onto waxed paper and rub it onto the bottom, sides, and corners inside a baking dish. Or, spray the inside of the dish with nonstick vegetable spray coating.

Cutting
Ask an adult to help you use a sharp knife and a cutting board to slice or chop vegetables, meat, or fruit. Be sure to chop foods into equal-size pieces so they will micro-cook evenly.

Shredding
Place the shredder over waxed paper to catch the food as you shred it. With adult help, hold the shredder in one hand. Use the other hand to push the food down along the side with the biggest holes, cutting the food into long, thin pieces. To finely shred food, use the side with the smallest holes.

Measuring Dry Ingredients
Use a dry measuring cup or spoon exactly the size you need. Put the ingredient into the cup or spoon, then level it off with a narrow metal spatula or the flat side of a table knife.
    To measure brown sugar, pack it into the measuring cup so it holds the shape when you dump it out.

Cracking Eggs
Hold an egg over a container. Use a table knife to crack the egg. With two hands, separate the shell halves over the container so the egg falls into the container. Remove any pieces of eggshell from the container. To beat the egg, stir it with a fork until the yolk and the white are mixed.

Hot Strawberry Malted

EQUIPMENT

measuring cups	ice cream scoop
measuring spoon	hot pads
rubber scraper	2 12-ounce mugs

¾ **cup milk**
1 **tablespoon instant malted milk powder**
1 **cup strawberry ice cream**

● Pour the milk into a 4-cup liquid measuring cup. Use a rubber scraper to stir in the malted milk powder. Add 1 cup ice cream. Do not cover. Place in the microwave oven; set on full or high (100%) power. Set the timer for 3 minutes. Start oven. After 3 minutes, stir. Micro-cook, uncovered, on high for 30 seconds to 1 minute more or till the ice cream is melted and the mixture is hot.

1 **cup strawberry ice cream**
Strawberry *or* vanilla ice cream (if you like)

● Divide 1 cup ice cream between two 12-ounce mugs. Pour the hot mixture over ice cream. Top with an additional scoop of strawberry or vanilla ice cream, if you like. Makes 2 (10-ounce) servings.

For a delicious milk shake that will tickle your tongue, try this melting ice cream treat. Heat half of the ice cream in your microwave oven. Then put the other half into mugs and pour the hot drink over it.

Spicy Cranberry-Apple Steamer

EQUIPMENT

measuring cups	small spoon
measuring spoon	8-ounce mug
hot pads	

½ **cup cranberry juice cocktail**
¼ **cup apple juice *or* apple cider**
2 **teaspoons red cinnamon candies**

● Put the cranberry juice, the apple juice or cider, and the red cinnamon candies into a 2-cup liquid measuring cup. Do not cover. Place in the microwave oven; set on full or high (100%) power. Set the timer for 2 minutes and 30 seconds. Start oven. After cooking, use a small spoon to stir. Pour into an 8-ounce mug. Let the drink stand 5 minutes before drinking. Makes 1 (6½-ounce) serving.

What's colorful, spicy, quick to fix, and delicious to sip? You'll know the answer as soon as you try this drink. You have to micro-cook it longer than some drinks so the cinnamon candies have time to melt. Stir the hot drink well, then let it cool a few minutes before you take your first sip.

Hot Strawberry Malted

Minty Malted Milk

EQUIPMENT

measuring cup	table knife
mug	small spoon
measuring spoon	hot pads

¾ **cup milk**
2 **tablespoons chocolate instant malted milk powder**
4 *or* 5 **pastel pillow mints**

● Pour the milk into a nonmetal mug. Add the chocolate malted milk powder; use a small spoon to stir. Put in the mints. Do not cover. Place in the microwave oven; set on full or high (100%) power. Set the timer for 1 minute. Start oven. If the drink is not hot after 1 minute, micro-cook, uncovered, on high for 30 seconds more. Stir before sipping. Makes 1 (6-ounce) serving.

Chocolate malted milk powder and colorful mints make this hot chocolate drink something extra special. The pink, yellow, and green mints are the kind restaurants sometimes serve after dinner. If you don't have any at home, look for them in the candy section of the supermarket.

Peanut Butter Mug Puddle

EQUIPMENT

measuring spoons	small spoon
table knife	measuring cup
mug	hot pads

2 **tablespoons creamy peanut butter**
2 **tablespoons chocolate-flavored syrup**
⅔ **cup milk**

● Put the peanut butter and the chocolate-flavored syrup into a nonmetal mug. Use a small spoon to stir till mixed. Stir in the milk. Do not cover. Place in the microwave oven; set on full or high (100%) power. Set the timer for 1 minute. Start oven. If the drink is not hot after 1 minute, micro-cook, uncovered, on high for 30 seconds more. Stir before sipping. Makes 1 (8-ounce) serving.

If you like chocolate and peanut butter flavors together, you won't be able to resist a hot mugful of this creamy treat.

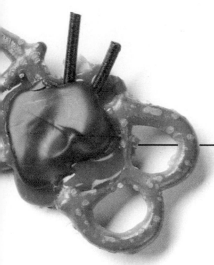

Fluttering Butterflies

EQUIPMENT

measuring cups	ruler
2 plastic bags	table knife
cutting board	hot pads
meat mallet	wooden spoon
waxed paper	small spoon
baking sheet	kitchen scissors
measuring spoons	container

Watch twisted pretzels and licorice turn into fluttering butterfly wings and antennae right before your eyes! A yummy caramel mixture and chocolate hold all the pieces together. After you press licorice into the caramel, you can lift the wings to make the butterflies look as if they are flying.

¼ cup nuts

● Put nuts into a plastic bag inside a second plastic bag. Close bags; set on a cutting board. Use a meat mallet to finely crush nuts. Set the nuts aside.

Butter *or* margarine
48 small twisted pretzels

● Grease a large baking sheet. For the base of *each* butterfly, sprinkle about ½ *teaspoon* of the crushed nuts in a small circle on baking sheet (1). Measure 2 inches between circles. Make *each* butterfly's wings by arranging *2* pretzels together (2) on top of nuts. Set aside.

1

½ of a 14-ounce package (about 25) vanilla and chocolate caramels
1 tablespoon milk
1 tablespoon butter *or* margarine

● Unwrap caramels. Put caramels, milk, and butter into a 4-cup liquid measuring cup. Do not cover. Place in microwave oven; set on full or high (100%) power. Set for 1 minute and 30 seconds. Start. After cooking, stir with a wooden spoon. If not soft enough to stir smooth, micro-cook, uncovered, on high for 30 seconds to 1 minute more. Spoon *1 teaspoon* mixture on *each* two pretzels (3). (Push caramel off teaspoon with small spoon.)

48 inches red *or* black shoestring licorice

● Use kitchen scissors to cut licorice into 1-inch-long pieces. Press *2* pieces into *each* butterfly (4). Chill, uncovered, in refrigerator 30 minutes or till firm.

2

½ of a 6-ounce package (½ cup) semisweet chocolate pieces

● Put chocolate pieces into a 2-cup liquid measuring cup. Micro-cook, uncovered, on high for 1 minute to 1 minute and 30 seconds or till melted. Spoon about ½ *teaspoon* chocolate onto *each* butterfly (5). Chill about 15 minutes or till chocolate is firm. Store in a single layer in a tightly covered container in the refrigerator. Makes 24 butterflies.

5

3

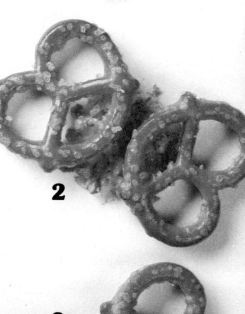

4

Crunchy Coated Banana Pops

EQUIPMENT

large tray	hot pads
waxed paper	rubber scraper
measuring cups	table knife
plastic bag	8 wooden sticks
rolling pin	foil

Have you ever tried making a banana snack on a stick? It's no trick at all. Just push sticks into banana halves, then coat the halves with peanut butter-flavored chocolate and crushed granola.

To crush the granola, push down hard on the rolling pin. You need to crush the granola fine enough to stick to the melted chocolate.

1½ cups plain granola

● Cover the top of a large tray with waxed paper. Put granola into a plastic bag. Close bag. Use a rolling pin to crush. Spread crushed granola in the center of the tray. Set granola aside.

1 6-ounce package (1 cup) milk chocolate pieces *or* semisweet chocolate pieces
⅓ cup creamy peanut butter

● Put chocolate pieces into a 4-cup liquid measuring cup. Do not cover. Place in microwave oven; set on full or high (100%) power. Set timer for 2 minutes. Start oven. Use a rubber scraper to stir. If pieces aren't soft enough to stir smooth, micro-cook for 30 seconds more. Add peanut butter; stir till smooth.

4 large bananas, cut in half crosswise

● Push a wooden stick into the cut end of each banana half. Use a table knife to spread chocolate mixture over each banana half, then roll in crushed granola. Set each coated banana at the side of the tray while working on the next. Chill the coated bananas in the freezer about 2 hours or till firm. Wrap each in foil. Store in the freezer. Makes 8 servings.

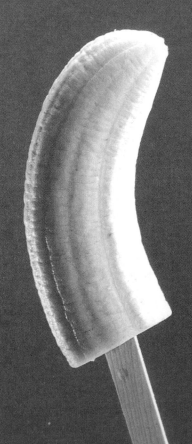

Rocky Road Pops

EQUIPMENT

measuring cups	hot pads
2 plastic bags	12 3-ounce paper
cutting board	cups
meat mallet	baking sheet
rubber scraper	12 wooden sticks

These frozen treats may remind you of rocky road ice cream, because the nuts and marshmallows make bumps in the rich chocolate. To keep the pops fresh-tasting and creamy, put each one into a small plastic bag after it's frozen. Then return the pops to the freezer.

⅓ cup peanuts

● Put the peanuts into a plastic bag inside a second plastic bag. Close the bags. Set on a cutting board. Use a meat mallet to crush the peanuts. Set aside.

2½ cups milk
1 package 4-serving-size *regular* chocolate pudding mix

● Pour milk into a 4-cup liquid measuring cup. Add pudding mix. Use a rubber scraper to stir till mix is dissolved. Do not cover. Place in the microwave oven; set on full or high (100%) power. Set the timer for 3 minutes. Start oven. After 3 minutes, stir from the outside to the center. Micro-cook, uncovered, on high for 2 to 3 minutes more or till slightly thickened. Stir again.

¾ cup tiny marshmallows
½ of a 6-ounce package (½ cup) miniature semi-sweet chocolate pieces

● Stir the marshmallows, chocolate, and chopped peanuts into the pudding. (The marshmallows and chocolate pieces will not melt completely.)

● Pour about *⅓ cup* of the pudding mixture into *each* paper cup. Put the filled cups onto a baking sheet. Chill in the freezer for 15 minutes. Put a wooden stick into the center of each chilled cup. Chill in the freezer about 5 hours more or till firm. To serve, peel off the paper cups. Makes 12 pops.

Hopscotcher's Squares

EQUIPMENT

8x8x2-inch baking dish	can opener
foil	2 rubber scrapers
waxed paper	hot pads
kitchen scissors	wooden spoon
measuring cups	measuring spoon
large mixing bowl	table knife
	container

This candy is smooth and creamy, with a little crunch from the chunky peanut butter. After you have poured it into the pan, chill the mixture in the refrigerator. The candy will get firm, so you can cut it into squares.

Butter *or* margarine
1 12-ounce package (2 cups) butterscotch pieces
1½ cups tiny marshmallows
1 14-ounce can (1¼ cups) Eagle Brand sweetened condensed milk

● Line an 8x8x2-inch baking dish with foil, overlapping the edges to make handles. Grease the foil with butter or margarine. Set aside.

Use kitchen scissors to open the package of butterscotch pieces. Put the butterscotch pieces and tiny marshmallows into a large nonmetal mixing bowl.

Use a can opener to open the can of sweetened condensed milk. Use a rubber scraper to push the milk into the bowl. Do not cover.

● Place the bowl in the microwave oven; set on full or high (100%) power. Set the timer for 5 minutes. Start oven. After 5 minutes, use a wooden spoon to stir till the mixture is nearly smooth. (Press marshmallows against the side of the bowl with the back of the spoon to make them blend in more quickly.)

Use a clean rubber scraper to spread the hot mixture evenly in the greased foil-lined baking dish. Be sure to push the mixture into the corners, as shown.

⅔ cup chunk-style peanut butter
1 teaspoon vanilla

● Add the peanut butter and vanilla. Stir hard till the candy is well mixed. Pour the candy into the foil-lined baking dish. Use a clean rubber scraper to push the candy into the corners and make the top of the candy smooth, as shown. Cover and chill in the refrigerator about 2 hours or till firm.

● To serve, lift the candy and the foil lining out of the baking dish, as shown. Use a table knife to cut the candy into 48 squares. Store any leftover candy in a tightly covered container in the refrigerator. Makes 48 squares.

It's as easy as playing hopscotch to remove the candy from the dish. Just lift the uncut candy out by holding the overlapping foil edges, as shown.

Somethin' More S'Mores

EQUIPMENT

table knife	measuring spoons
cutting board	hot pads
small plate	

2 graham cracker squares
½ of a 1- to 1.5-ounce bar milk chocolate
2 maraschino cherries, cut into fourths
1 large marshmallow, cut in half

Chocolate-Cherry S'More: On a nonmetal plate top *1* cracker with chocolate, cherries, marshmallow, and remaining cracker. Do not cover. Place in microwave oven. Micro-cook on full or high (100%) power for 10 to 15 seconds. Let stand 30 to 60 seconds. Makes 1.

2 graham cracker squares
½ of a 1- to 1.5-ounce bar milk chocolate
1 teaspoon almond brickle pieces
1 large marshmallow, cut in half

English Toffee S'More: On a nonmetal plate top *1* cracker with chocolate, almond brickle pieces, marshmallow, and remaining cracker. Do not cover. Place in microwave oven; set on full or high (100%) power. Set timer for 10 to 15 seconds. Start oven. Let stand for 30 to 60 seconds. Makes 1.

2 graham cracker squares
½ of a 1- to 1.5-ounce bar milk chocolate
4 thin slices banana
1 large marshmallow, cut in half

Bits of Banana S'More: On a nonmetal plate top *1* cracker with chocolate, banana slices, marshmallow, and remaining cracker. Do not cover. Place in microwave oven; set on full or high (100%) power. Set the timer for 10 to 15 seconds. Start oven. Let stand for 30 to 60 seconds. Makes 1 serving.

2 graham cracker squares
2 teaspoons peanut butter
½ of a 1- to 1.5-ounce bar milk chocolate
1 large marshmallow, cut in half

Nutty S'More: On a nonmetal plate spread *1* cracker with peanut butter. Add chocolate, marshmallow, and remaining cracker. Do not cover. Place in the microwave oven. Micro-cook on full or high (100%) power for 10 to 15 seconds. Let stand 30 to 60 seconds. Makes 1.

2 graham cracker squares
½ of a 1- to 1.5-ounce bar milk chocolate with crisped rice
1 large marshmallow, cut in half

Crisp Crackly S'More: On a nonmetal plate top *1* cracker with chocolate, marshmallow, and remaining cracker. Do not cover. Place in microwave oven; set on full or high (100%) power. Set timer for 10 to 15 seconds. Start oven. Let stand for 30 to 60 seconds. Makes 1.

2 graham cracker squares
1 cream-filled chocolate-covered peppermint patty
1 large marshmallow, cut in half

Melting Mint S'More: On a nonmetal plate top *1* cracker with the patty, marshmallow, and remaining cracker. Do not cover. Place in microwave oven; set on full or high (100%) power. Set timer for 10 to 15 seconds. Start oven. Let stand for 30 to 60 seconds. Makes 1.

If your oven has a window you can see through, watch the marshmallow as it micro-cooks—it will grow bigger and bigger. And when you take the s'more from the oven, the marshmallow will flatten like a leaky balloon.

The chocolate still may seem hard after micro-cooking. But you'll find that if you let the s'more stand for a few seconds, the chocolate will melt just the way it should.

Pearadise Topper

EQUIPMENT

can opener	table knife
strainer	hot pads
medium mixing	toaster *or*
bowl	ice cream scoop
measuring spoons	small plate *or*
rubber scraper	bowl
cutting board	large spoon

We asked our kid-friends what time of day they'd like to eat this full-of-fruit sauce. Kelly decided she'd want to eat it after school, on top of a waffle. Chris said he'd like the same thing, but for breakfast. The others thought they'd eat it on ice cream for dessert. But they all agreed on one thing—this pear sauce makes a great-tasting hunger-stopper.

---

1 8-ounce can pear halves (juice pack)
1 teaspoon cornstarch
¼ teaspoon ground cinnamon
2 tablespoons raisins

● Use a can opener to open the can of pears. Put a strainer onto a medium nonmetal mixing bowl. Pour the pear halves into the strainer so the juice drains into the bowl. Set the pears aside. Use a rubber scraper to stir the cornstarch and the cinnamon into the juice. On a cutting board use a table knife to chop pears. Put the pears into the bowl. Stir in raisins. Do not cover.

● Place the bowl in the microwave oven; set on full or high (100%) power. Set the timer for 1 minute. Start oven. After 1 minute, stir. Micro-cook, uncovered, on high for 1 to 2 minutes more or till the topper is thickened and bubbly. Stir the topper again.

---

1 frozen waffle *or* vanilla ice cream

● Toast the waffle in a toaster. Put the waffle onto a small plate. (*Or,* put the ice cream into a small bowl.) Use a large spoon to put some of the warm topper over the waffle or the ice cream. Store the remaining topper in a tightly covered container in the refrigerator. Makes about 1¼ cups sauce.

You'll probably have enough topper that you can save some for later. To reheat, micro-cook ½ cup pear topper, uncovered, on high for 30 seconds or till hot.

Right Now Nachos

EQUIPMENT

9-inch pie plate	measuring cup
measuring spoon	hot pads

18 tortilla chips 1 tablespoon taco sauce ¼ cup shredded cheddar cheese	● Arrange tortilla chips in a 9-inch nonmetal pie plate. Drizzle a few drops of taco sauce over each chip. Sprinkle cheese over chips. Do not cover. Place in the microwave oven; set on full or high (100%) power. Set the timer for 30 seconds. Start oven. If the cheese is not melted after 30 seconds, micro-cook, uncovered, on high for 5 to 10 seconds more. Let stand for 1 minute before eating. Makes 18.

Are you hungry and in the mood for something deliciously cheesy right now? We think you will agree with Aaron and Sarah—you can't beat these nachos!

The cheese gets very hot as it micro-cooks, so wait a minute before you take your first bite.

Cheesy Potato Sticks

EQUIPMENT

vegetable brush	9-inch pie plate
sharp knife	hot pads
cutting board	waxed paper
table knife	fork
ruler	measuring spoons

3 medium potatoes	● Use a vegetable brush to scrub the potatoes. Ask an adult to help you cut each potato lengthwise into 8 wedges. (*Or,* cut into ½-inch-thick slices.)
2 tablespoons butter *or* margarine	● Put butter into a 9-inch nonmetal pie plate. Do not cover. Place in microwave oven; set on full or high (100%) power. Set timer for 15 seconds. Start oven. After 15 seconds, if not melted, micro-cook on high for 15 to 30 seconds more.
2 tablespoons grated Parmesan cheese Chili powder *or* paprika (if you like)	● Dip potato wedges or slices into melted butter to coat. Place, peel side down, in pie plate. Cover with waxed paper. Micro-cook on high for 5 minutes. Use hot pads to turn dish halfway around. Micro-cook 5 to 6 minutes more or till potatoes are tender when you poke them with a fork. Sprinkle with cheese and chili powder, if you like. Let stand, covered, for 5 minutes. Serves 4.

A little like French fries, a little like potato skins, these make a hearty snack that will really fill you up. Try them with a meal, too.

The chili powder will add color as well as flavor, but sprinkle on just a little—it's hot!

One Potato, Two Potato...

EQUIPMENT

vegetable brush	measuring cups
fork	wooden spoon
shallow baking dish	kitchen scissors
hot pads	*or* can opener
foil	sharp knife
table knife	cutting board
small spoon	waxed paper
large mixing bowl	plastic bag
potato masher	rolling pin

4 medium baking potatoes

● Scrub potatoes. Prick with a fork. Put into a shallow nonmetal baking dish. Do not cover. Place in the microwave oven; set on full or high (100%) power. Set timer for 12 minutes. After 12 minutes, cover dish with foil; let stand 5 minutes.

**Pizza Filling *or*
Taco Filling**

● Remove the foil; let potatoes stand till cool enough to handle. Slice off the tops. Ask an adult to help you spoon out the centers, leaving shells. Put the potato centers into a large mixing bowl and mash. Choose a filling; finish making and cooking as directed. Makes 4 servings.

Pizza Filling:
¼ **cup milk**
2 **ounces sliced pepperoni, salami, *or* fully cooked ham**
½ **of a medium green pepper**
Pizza sauce *or* spaghetti sauce
Grated Parmesan cheese

Stir milk into mashed potatoes. Use kitchen scissors to cut up pepperoni, salami, or ham. Ask an adult to help you chop green pepper. Stir meat and pepper into mashed potatoes. Spoon into potato shells. Return to baking dish. Cover with waxed paper. Micro-cook on high about 5 minutes or till hot. After cooking, top with pizza sauce or spaghetti sauce and Parmesan cheese.

Taco Filling:
¼ **cup milk**
1 **8-ounce can red kidney beans**
¼ **cup shredded cheddar cheese (1 ounce)**
Taco-flavored tortilla chips
Taco sauce
Dairy sour cream (if you like)

Stir milk into mashed potatoes. Open the can of beans; drain. Stir beans and shredded cheddar cheese into mashed potatoes. Spoon into potato shells. Return to baking dish. Cover with waxed paper. Micro-cook on high for 4 to 5 minutes or till hot. Meanwhile, put the tortilla chips into a plastic bag and use a rolling pin to crush them. Top the potatoes with taco sauce, crushed chips, and sour cream, if you like.

What can you do when you and your friends are really hungry between meals? We've got the answer—make a jazzed-up potato! Choose a pizza potato or a taco potato, made special with a combination of flavorful fillers and toppers.

You can bake four potatoes in just 12 minutes in the microwave oven. After micro-cooking, cover the potatoes with foil to hold the heat in, so the potatoes will continue to cook. Be careful when you remove the foil—these are hot potatoes!

Get-Up-and-Go Granola

EQUIPMENT

measuring cups	table knife
measuring spoons	fork
large mixing bowl	hot pads
wooden spoon	container

This is no ordinary granola! You mix in mashed banana before micro-cooking, for a flavor our kid testers said is "like oatmeal cookies." For a snack, grab a handful of this good-for-you energy booster instead of bubble gum or candy. Or, have it for breakfast with milk and your favorite fruit.

1½ cups regular rolled oats ⅓ cup toasted wheat germ *or* sesame seed ⅓ cup packed brown sugar ¼ cup coconut ¼ cup sliced almonds ¼ teaspoon ground cinnamon	● Put the oats, wheat germ or sesame seed, brown sugar, coconut, almonds, and cinnamon into a large nonmetal mixing bowl. Use a wooden spoon to stir till well mixed. Set the mixture aside.
1 small banana ¼ cup cooking oil 1 teaspoon vanilla	● Use a table knife to slice the banana into a 1-cup liquid measuring cup. Use a fork to mash the banana till nearly smooth. (There should be about ¼ cup mashed banana.) Add the cooking oil and vanilla. Stir till well mixed. Pour the banana-oil mixture over the oat mixture. Stir till the oat mixture is coated with the banana-oil mixture. Do not cover.
	● Place in the microwave oven; set on full or high (100%) power. Set the timer for 3 minutes. Start oven. After 3 minutes, stir the mixture from the outside to the center. Micro-cook, uncovered, on high for 3 minutes more. Stir again. Micro-cook, uncovered, on high for 2 minutes more.
½ cup chopped mixed dried fruit *or* raisins	● Stir in the dried fruit or raisins. Let the granola cool for 1 hour, stirring once. Store in a tightly covered container for up to 2 weeks. Makes about 4 cups.

Noisy Nibble Mix

EQUIPMENT

table knife	2 rubber scrapers
measuring cups	large shallow pan
large mixing bowl	container
hot pads	

¼ **cup butter *or* margarine**
¼ **cup chunk-style peanut butter**

● Put the butter or margarine and peanut butter into a large nonmetal mixing bowl. Do not cover. Place in the microwave oven; set on full or high (100%) power. Set the timer for 1 minute and 30 seconds. Start oven. After 1 minute and 30 seconds, if the butter is not melted and the peanut butter is not soft, micro-cook, uncovered, on high for 30 seconds more. Use a rubber scraper to stir till well mixed.

5 **cups cereal (bite-size shredded corn, wheat, rice, *or* bran squares; bite-size shredded wheat biscuits; *or* round toasted oat cereal)**
1 **cup small twisted pretzels**
1 **cup peanuts**
1 **cup sunflower nuts**

● Add the cereal, pretzels, peanuts, and sunflower nuts to the peanut butter mixture. Toss gently with 2 rubber scrapers till the cereal mixture is coated with the peanut butter mixture. Micro-cook, uncovered, on high for 6 minutes. Stir *after 2 minutes* and *after 4 minutes.* Spread the mix in a large shallow pan to cool. Store in a tightly covered container. Makes about 7½ cups mix.

You can't be sneaky about eating this crispy combination of cereal, pretzels, and nuts. Everyone who hears you munching will want to try it. But watch out—it tastes so peanut-buttery good, they just might not want to stop!

Nutty Crunchers

EQUIPMENT

toaster	waxed paper
cutting board	measuring spoon
table knife	hot pads
ruler	rubber scraper
measuring cups	small plate
plastic bag	cooling rack
rolling pin	

At first, Amy thought the peanut-butter-covered toast sticks would be too gooey to pick up. But after she coated them in cereal and let them cool, she found they were crispy, crunchy, and easy to eat.

---

2 slices whole wheat bread

● Toast the whole wheat bread in a toaster. On a cutting board use a table knife to cut each slice into four 1-inch-wide sticks, making 8 sticks. Set aside.

---

1 cup corn flakes

● Put the corn flakes into a plastic bag. Close the bag. Use a rolling pin or your hands to crush the corn flakes. Spread the crushed corn flakes in a thick layer on a piece of waxed paper.

¼ cup creamy peanut butter
1 tablespoon cooking oil

● Put the peanut butter and oil into a 2-cup liquid measuring cup. Do not cover. Place in the microwave oven; set on full or high (100%) power. Set the timer for 1 minute. Start oven. After 1 minute, stir with a rubber scraper. Scrape the mixture onto a small plate. Roll the toast sticks in the peanut butter mixture, as shown. Hold each coated toast stick above the peanut butter mixture so the excess drips onto the plate. Roll in the crushed corn flakes, as shown. Put the sticks onto a cooling rack to cool. Makes 8 sticks.

Scrape the hot peanut butter mixture onto a small plate. Roll one stick at a time in the mixture, as shown. Let the excess drip onto the plate.

Roll each toast stick in the crushed corn flakes to completely cover the toast with the cereal, as shown. Cool the coated sticks on a cooling rack.

Upside-Down Apple Cake

EQUIPMENT

sharp knife	measuring spoons
cutting board	small mixing bowl
table knife	medium mixing
12x7½x2-inch	bowl
baking dish	rubber scraper
hot pads	toothpick
waxed paper	cooling rack
2 forks	serving platter
measuring cups	ice cream scoop

This cake really does get turned upside down. Arrange the apples in a pattern in the baking dish before you add the batter. When you turn the cake out of the dish, the pattern will be on top.

2 medium apples

● Ask an adult to help you core each apple. To core, push knife into top close to stem. Cut all the way around stem. Turn apple upside down and repeat. Pull out core. Thinly slice apples.

¼ cup butter *or* margarine

● Put butter into a 12x7½x2-inch nonmetal baking dish. Do not cover. Place in microwave oven; set on full or high (100%) power. Set timer for 30 seconds. Start oven. If not melted, micro-cook 15 to 30 seconds more. Arrange apple slices evenly in dish; cover with waxed paper. Micro-cook 3 to 4 minutes or till tender when poked with a fork.

Carefully pour the batter into the dish, as shown, so the apples don't move.

⅓ cup packed brown sugar
¼ teaspoon ground cinnamon

● Put the brown sugar and cinnamon into a small mixing bowl. Use the fork to stir. Sprinkle over the apple slices.

1 egg
1 cup water
1 tablespoon cooking oil
1 14½-ounce package gingerbread mix
½ cup raisins (if you like)

● Use a table knife to crack egg; open and pour into a medium mixing bowl. Stir with a clean fork. Stir in water and oil. Add gingerbread mix and raisins, if you like. Use a rubber scraper to stir just till mix is wet, but still lumpy. Set aside.

● Micro-cook apples, uncovered, on high about 1 minute or till hot. Carefully pour gingerbread mixture evenly into dish without moving apples, as shown. Do not cover. Micro-cook on high for 9 minutes or till most of the top looks dry, using hot pads to turn dish one-quarter of the way around *after 3 minutes* and *after 6 minutes.* Test with a toothpick, as shown. If crumbs stick to pick, micro-cook for 1 minute more.

To see if the cake is done, use a toothpick to scrape away the top from a wet-looking patch. The cake should be dry underneath. Push the pick halfway down, then pull it out, as shown. If the toothpick comes out clean, the cake is done.

Vanilla ice cream (if you like)

● Let cool on a cooling rack 5 minutes. Ask an adult to help you invert cake onto a serving platter. Serve warm with ice cream, if you like. Makes 12 servings.

Apple and Peanut Butter Cake

EQUIPMENT

sharp knife	rubber scraper
vegetable peeler	small bowl
cutting board	8x1½-inch
measuring cups	round baking
measuring spoons	dish
small mixing bowl	toothpick
2 forks	cooling rack
table knife	sifter
2 medium mixing	large mixing bowl
bowls	narrow metal
hot pads	spatula

Jenny made this recipe, so she knew there was a chopped-up apple in the batter. But none of the other kids could taste the apple, so they wondered why it was there. What's the answer? The apple makes these snack bars moist and combines with the other ingredients for extra flavor.

---

1 small apple
⅓ cup all-purpose flour
¼ cup whole wheat flour
¾ teaspoon baking powder

● Ask an adult to help you core the apple. To core, push knife into top close to stem. Cut all the way around stem. Turn apple upside down and repeat. Pull core out. Peel and chop apple. Put flours and baking powder into a small mixing bowl. Use a fork to stir. Set aside.

⅓ cup creamy peanut butter
¼ cup butter *or* margarine
¾ cup packed brown sugar

● Put peanut butter and butter into a medium nonmetal mixing bowl. Do not cover. Place in microwave oven; set on full or high (100%) power. Set for 30 seconds. Start oven. Stir with a rubber scraper till mixed. Stir in brown sugar.

---

2 eggs
⅓ cup milk
1 teaspoon vanilla
⅓ cup quick-cooking rolled oats

● Use a table knife to crack eggs; open and pour into a small bowl. Add eggs, milk, and vanilla to the peanut butter mixture; stir. Stir in the flour mixture. Add oats and apple; stir. Spread the mixture into an 8x1½-inch round nonmetal baking dish. Do not cover.
  Micro-cook on high for 8 minutes, using hot pads to turn the dish halfway around *after 4 minutes*. Test with a toothpick, as shown. If crumbs stick to pick, micro-cook for 1 minute more. Let cool on a cooling rack for 1 hour.

---

1 cup powdered sugar
½ of a 3-ounce package cream cheese
2 tablespoons creamy peanut butter
1 to 2 tablespoons milk
½ teaspoon vanilla

● For frosting, use a sifter to sift powdered sugar into a large mixing bowl. Measure 1 cup; set aside. Put cream cheese and peanut butter into a clean medium nonmetal mixing bowl. Micro-cook, uncovered, 30 seconds. Stir till smooth. Stir in *half* of the sugar, *2 teaspoons* of the milk, and vanilla. Stir in remaining sugar and enough milk to make frosting thin enough to spread. Use a narrow metal spatula to spread frosting onto cake. Makes 12 servings.

Sunshine in a Pocket

EQUIPMENT

sharp knife	measuring cups
cutting board	measuring spoons
table knife	hot pads
1-quart casserole	rubber scraper
fork	small spoon

Cheesy scrambled eggs for breakfast will start your day shining, no matter what the weather. Serve them in a pita pocket and you won't even need a fork.

1 medium tomato
2 large pita bread rounds

● Ask an adult to help you use a sharp knife and a cutting board to chop the tomato. Throw away the seeds. Slice the bread in half to make pockets. Set aside.

6 eggs

● Use a table knife to crack each egg; open and pour into a 1-quart nonmetal casserole. Stir with a fork to mix.

⅓ cup milk
¼ teaspoon salt
¼ teaspoon pepper

● Stir the milk, salt, and pepper into the eggs. Do not cover. Place in the microwave oven; set on full or high (100%) power. Set the timer for 4 minutes. Start oven. *After each minute,* use a rubber scraper to push the outside cooked portion to the center. After 4 minutes, if the eggs are too runny, micro-cook, uncovered, on high for 10 seconds to 1 minute more.

3 slices American cheese

● Tear the cheese into small pieces. Sprinkle the cheese over the eggs. Micro-cook, uncovered, on high for 1 to 2 minutes or till melted, stirring once.

The eggs should still be a little runny when you add the cheese. They'll finish cooking while the cheese is melting.

Alfalfa sprouts *or* torn lettuce leaves

● To serve, use a spoon to fill *each* pita bread pocket with about *½ cup* of the egg mixture. Top the filled pockets with the alfalfa sprouts or lettuce and chopped tomato. Makes 4 servings.

Log and Barrel Scramble

On our taste panel, Pam said the sausages reminded her of chopped trees. And Janelle thought the potatoes looked like barrels. That's how we came up with the name for this dish.

EQUIPMENT

measuring cups	medium mixing
9-inch pie plate	bowl
hot pads	fork
large spoon	measuring spoons
table knife	cutting board
	rubber scraper

1½ **cups frozen fried potato nuggets**

● Put the potato nuggets into a 9-inch nonmetal pie plate. Do not cover. Place in the microwave oven; set on full or high (100%) power. Set the timer for 4 minutes. Start oven. After 4 minutes, if the nuggets are not hot, micro-cook, uncovered, for 10 seconds to 1 minute more. Use a large spoon to remove the nuggets from the dish. Set aside.

1 **tablespoon butter *or* margarine**

● Put the butter or margarine into the hot dish. Micro-cook, uncovered, on high for 15 to 30 seconds or till melted.

4 **eggs**
¼ **cup milk**
1 **teaspoon dried parsley flakes**
¼ **teaspoon salt**
Dash pepper

● Use the table knife to crack each egg; open and pour into a mixing bowl. Stir with a fork. Stir in the milk, parsley flakes, salt, and pepper. Pour the mixture over the melted butter in the pie plate.

2 **fully cooked smoked sausage links**

● On a cutting board use the table knife to slice the sausage links crosswise. Add the sausage pieces to the egg mixture. Micro-cook, uncovered, on high for 3 minutes. *After every minute,* use a rubber scraper to push the uncooked egg from the outside to the center.

● Arrange potato nuggets on top of the egg mixture, around the edge of the dish. Micro-cook, uncovered, on high about 1 minute more or till eggs are set but still shiny. Makes 4 servings.

Full-of-Baloney French Toast

EQUIPMENT

table knife	hot pads
plate	measuring cup

2 slices frozen French toast Butter *or* margarine	● Use a table knife to spread one side of each slice of frozen French toast with butter or margarine.
1 slice bologna *or* fully cooked ham 1 slice Swiss *or* American cheese	● Put 1 slice of French toast, buttered side up, onto a nonmetal plate. Put the bologna or ham and the cheese on top. Add the remaining slice of French toast, buttered side down. Do not cover.
	● Place the plate in the microwave oven; set on full or high (100%) power. Set the timer for 1 minute. Start oven. After 1 minute, if the cheese is not melted, micro-cook, uncovered, on high for 10 seconds to 1 minute more.
Maple-flavored syrup	● If you like, heat the syrup by pouring ¼ cup syrup into a 1-cup liquid measuring cup. Micro-cook, uncovered, on high for 30 to 45 seconds or till warm. To serve, pour as much syrup as you want over the warm sandwich. Makes 1 serving.

When people say you're "full of baloney," they usually mean you're telling a tall tale. But you don't need to kid anyone into trying this cheesy French toast sandwich.

If you don't want to make it full of bologna, you can always ham it up with ham. Whatever you do, we suggest you eat this sandwich with a knife and fork because the syrup is sticky.

Bacon Barber Poles

EQUIPMENT

toaster	microwave bacon
cutting board	rack *or* plate
table knife	white paper towel
ruler	hot pads
kitchen scissors	tongs

Have you ever seen a striped pole outside a barber shop? Then you'll understand how we named these bacon-wrapped toast sticks. Micro-cook them for a crunchy breakfast side dish or for a snack.

1 slice whole wheat *or* white bread

● Toast the bread in a toaster. On a cutting board use a table knife and a ruler to cut the toast into 1-inch-wide sticks, making 4 sticks.

2 slices bacon

● Use kitchen scissors to cut each slice of bacon lengthwise into 2 strips, making 4 strips. Wrap 1 bacon strip around each toast stick in a spiral, as shown.

● Put the toast sticks onto a nonmetal bacon rack or a *white* paper towel on a nonmetal plate. Cover with a *white* paper towel. Place in the microwave oven; set on full or high (100%) power. Set the timer for 1 minute. Start oven. After 1 minute, use hot pads and tongs to turn sticks over. Micro-cook, covered, on high for 1 minute more. If bacon is not crisp, micro-cook, covered, on high for 10 seconds to 1 minute more. Makes 4.

After you cut the bacon slices in half lengthwise, wrap each bacon strip around one stick of toast in a spiral, as shown.

Plump Raisin Porridge

EQUIPMENT measuring spoons measuring cups 2 plastic bags table knife cutting board small spoon meat mallet waxed paper cereal bowl hot pads	**You'll warm up quickly on frosty mornings when you make our cinnamon-flavored oatmeal. The raisins or dried fruit get really plump as they cook in the microwave oven.**

1 tablespoon nuts (if you like)

● If you want to use nuts, put them into a plastic bag, then into a second plastic bag. Close the bags. On a cutting board use a meat mallet to crush. Set aside.

¼ cup quick-cooking rolled oats
2 tablespoons raisins *or* chopped mixed dried fruit
2 teaspoons brown sugar
⅛ teaspoon ground cinnamon
½ cup water

● In a nonmetal cereal bowl put the oats, raisins or mixed dried fruit, brown sugar, and cinnamon. Use a small spoon to stir the mixture. Stir in the water. Cover with waxed paper.

● Place the bowl in the microwave oven; set on full or high (100%) power. Set the timer for 1 minute and 30 seconds. Start oven. After 1 minute and 30 seconds, if the water is not absorbed, micro-cook, covered, on high for 15 seconds more. Let stand, covered, for 5 minutes to finish cooking.

2 to 3 tablespoons milk

● *Carefully* remove the cover. Stir in the milk till creamy. Top with the crushed nuts, if you like. Makes 1 serving.

Goofy Gooey Biscuits

EQUIPMENT

table knife	6 6-ounce custard
measuring cups	cups
hot pads	2 plastic bags
measuring spoon	cutting board
small spoon	meat mallet
	6 small plates

These gooey biscuits seem goofy when you're making them, but not when you're eating them! The chocolate and peanuts start out on the bottom but wind up on the top. After micro-cooking, you turn each custard cup upside down onto a plate, and the biscuit slips out. The chocolate syrup drips down over the sides of the biscuits. Watch out for sticky fingers!

2 tablespoons butter *or* margarine

● Put the butter or margarine into a 1-cup liquid measuring cup. Do not cover. Place in the microwave oven; set on full or high (100%) power. Set the timer for 15 seconds. Start oven. If the butter or margarine is not melted after 15 seconds, micro-cook, uncovered, on high for 15 to 30 seconds more.

¼ cup packed brown sugar
1 tablespoon chocolate-flavored syrup

● Use a spoon to stir the brown sugar and chocolate syrup into the melted butter. Spoon the mixture into six 6-ounce nonmetal custard cups.

¼ cup peanuts

● Put the peanuts into a plastic bag inside a second bag. Close the bags. On a cutting board use a meat mallet to crush nuts. Sprinkle crushed nuts over chocolate mixture in custard cups (1).

1 package (6) refrigerated biscuits

● Open the can of biscuits, following the package directions. Place one biscuit into each custard cup (2). Do not cover. Arrange custard cups in a circle in the microwave oven. Micro-cook on high for 2 minutes. After 2 minutes, if biscuits are not done, micro-cook, uncovered, on high for 10 seconds to 1 minute more.

● Cover each custard cup with an upside-down plate. Use hot pads to invert the custard cups onto the plates. Let stand for 1 minute, then remove the custard cups (3). Spoon any syrup left in the custard cups onto the biscuits. Serve warm. Makes 6 biscuits.

3

2

1

Surprising Peanut Butter Muffins

Also pictured on page 4.

Hide secret treats in these muffins and chances are, even you will be surprised by what's inside. Once you've micro-cooked them, will you remember which muffin holds which treat? We tried, and we couldn't remember!

If you have a microwave muffin pan, you can use it to micro-cook these muffins. The cooking times will be the same.

EQUIPMENT

measuring cups	rubber scraper
measuring spoons	6 6-ounce
medium mixing	custard cups
bowl	6 paper bake cups
fork	toothpick
table knife	hot pads
small mixing bowl	cooling rack

⅔ cup all-purpose flour 3 tablespoons brown sugar 1 teaspoon baking powder	● Put flour, 3 tablespoons brown sugar, and baking powder into medium mixing bowl. Use a fork to stir till well mixed.
1 egg ⅓ cup peanut butter ¼ cup milk 1 tablespoon cooking oil	● Use a table knife to crack the egg; open and pour into a small mixing bowl. Stir with the fork. Use a rubber scraper to stir in peanut butter, milk, and oil. (The mixture will not look well mixed.) Add the peanut butter mixture to flour mixture. Stir till dry ingredients are wet but still lumpy. Do not stir too much.
Jam, jelly, cream cheese, semisweet chocolate pieces, thinly sliced banana, *or* maraschino cherries Brown sugar	● Line custard cups with bake cups. Put *1 rounded tablespoon* of batter into *each* cup. Add *½ teaspoon* of jam, jelly, cream cheese, or chocolate pieces, or *1* banana slice or cherry. Top with *1 rounded tablespoon* of batter. Sprinkle additional brown sugar on top.
	● Arrange cups in a circle in center of microwave oven. Set on full or high (100%) power. Set timer for 2 minutes. Start. After 2 minutes, insert a toothpick near center of a muffin. If pick comes out clean, the muffin is done. If batter sticks to pick, micro-cook on high for 10 seconds to 1 minute more. When done, remove from cups. Cool on cooling rack 10 minutes; serve warm. Makes 6.

Microwave Heating Times for Breakfast Foods

What can you do on a hurried morning, when you don't have much time to make a hot breakfast? Just put any of these quick-to-fix breakfast foods into your microwave oven, and they'll be ready in the blink of an eye. Have a glass of your favorite juice and milk with your rolls, hot cereal, or French toast and you'll have enough steam to keep you going till lunch time.

Oatmeal: Put one 1- to 2-ounce package of *instant oatmeal* into a nonmetal cereal bowl. Stir in water, following package directions. Micro-cook, uncovered, on high for 1 minute to 1 minute and 30 seconds or till water is absorbed.

Bacon: Place 1 or 2 sheets of *white* paper towel in a shallow nonmetal baking dish. Arrange 2 slices of *bacon* on paper towel. Cover with a single layer of *white* paper towel. Micro-cook on high for 1 minute and 30 seconds to 2 minutes or till done. For 4 slices of bacon, micro-cook for 2 minutes and 30 seconds to 3 minutes.

French Toast: Put 2 slices of frozen *French toast* onto a large nonmetal plate. If you like, add a dab of *butter* or *margarine* and some *maple-flavored syrup*. Micro-cook, uncovered, on high for 1 minute to 1 minute and 15 seconds or till heated through. For 3 slices of frozen French toast, micro-cook, uncovered, on high for 1 minute and 30 seconds to 1 minute and 45 seconds or till heated through.

Muffins: Put 2 *muffins* onto a *white* paper towel on a nonmetal plate. Micro-cook, uncovered, on high for 15 to 20 seconds (if room temperature) or 40 to 50 seconds (if frozen). Micro-cook 4 muffins for 25 to 30 seconds (if room temperature) or 50 seconds to 1 minute (if frozen), turning once.

Cocoa: Put 1 envelope of *instant cocoa mix* and ⅔ cup *cold water* into a 10-ounce nonmetal mug; stir. Micro-cook, uncovered, on high for 1 minute to 1 minute and 30 seconds or till cocoa is hot.

Biscuits: Put 2 *biscuits* onto a *white* paper towel on a nonmetal plate. Micro-cook, uncovered, on high for 15 to 20 seconds (if room temperature) or 25 to 30 seconds (if frozen).

Sweet Rolls: Put 2 *sweet rolls* onto a *white* paper towel on a nonmetal plate. Micro-cook, uncovered, on high for 15 to 20 seconds (if room temperature) or 35 to 45 seconds (if frozen). For 4 sweet rolls, micro-cook for 25 to 30 seconds (if room temperature) or 1 minute to 1 minute and 10 seconds (if frozen), turning the plate halfway around once.

Cake Doughnuts: Put 2 *plain cake doughnuts* onto a *white* paper towel on a nonmetal plate. Micro-cook, uncovered, on high for 15 to 20 seconds (if room temperature) or 30 to 35 seconds (if frozen). For 4 doughnuts, micro-cook for 25 to 30 seconds (if room temperature) or 50 seconds to 1 minute (if frozen), turning the plate halfway around once during cooking.

Super Sloppy Joe

Also pictured on the cover.

EQUIPMENT

2 sharp knives	can opener
cutting board	rubber scraper
1½-quart casserole	measuring spoon
hot pads	small spoon
wooden spoon	ruler
long-handled spoon	plastic bag
container for fat	table knife

1 medium onion
1 medium tomato
1 pound ground beef

● Ask an adult to help you use a sharp knife and a cutting board to chop the onion. Chop tomato; throw away seeds. Set tomato aside. Use your hands to crumble beef into a 1½-quart nonmetal casserole; add onion. Do not cover.

● Place in microwave oven; set on full or high (100%) power. Set timer for 4 minutes. Start oven. *After 2 minutes,* use a wooden spoon to stir from the outside to center. After 4 minutes, if meat is not all brown, micro-cook, uncovered, for 15 seconds to 2 minutes more. Ask an adult to help you spoon off fat.

1 10¾-ounce can condensed tomato soup
½ of a 1¼-ounce envelope (2 tablespoons) taco seasoning mix

● Use a can opener to open the can of soup. Use a rubber scraper to scrape the soup into the meat. Stir in the seasoning mix. Cover with the lid. Micro-cook on high for 2 to 3 minutes or till hot. Ask an adult to help you remove the cover.

1 16-ounce loaf unsliced round bread or 6 to 8 hamburger buns

● Ask an adult to help you use a clean, sharp knife to slice loaf or buns in half crosswise; set bun halves aside. Use a spoon to hollow out top and bottom of loaf, leaving two 1-inch-thick shells. (Store bread from center of loaf in a plastic bag to use as bread crumbs.) Cut top shell into 6 to 8 wedges, if you like.

4 slices American cheese
Lettuce leaves

● Use a table knife to cut the cheese into triangles or strips. Set aside. Line bottom of bread shell or bun halves with lettuce. Spoon on meat mixture. Top with cheese and tomato. Cover with top bread shell, as shown, or wedges or bun halves. Makes 6 to 8 servings.

Fee, fie, foe, fum—here's a sandwich fit for a giant! Our taco-flavored sloppy Joe is so huge, it will feed you and five to seven other people. To make it easier to serve, you can cut the top of the big bun into wedges before putting it onto the filling, if you like.

If you don't have the big round loaf of bread, spoon the filling onto hamburger bun halves.

Curly Dogs and Beans

EQUIPMENT
can opener	measuring spoons
rubber scraper	cutting board
1½-quart casserole	table knife
measuring cup	hot pads

Watch these dogs curve into circles as they cook. Aaron, the excited young chef who made this recipe in our Test Kitchen, was peeking through his oven window as the hot dogs were cooking. His eyes grew wide and he shouted,"Hey, look! They're really curling!"

1 **16-ounce can pork and beans in tomato sauce**
¼ **cup bottled barbecue sauce**
2 **tablespoons brown sugar**
1 **teaspoon prepared mustard**
½ **teaspoon Worcestershire sauce**

● Use a can opener to open the beans. Use a rubber scraper to push the beans into a 1½-quart nonmetal casserole. Stir in the barbecue sauce, brown sugar, mustard, and Worcestershire sauce.

6 **hot dogs**

● On a cutting board use a table knife to slice *2* of the hot dogs crosswise. Stir the hot dog slices into the bean mixture. Make 4 small cuts crosswise on each remaining hot dog, cutting to, but not through, the opposite side, as shown. Set the slashed hot dogs aside.

● Cover bean mixture with the lid. Place in microwave oven; set on full or high (100%) power. Set timer for 4 minutes. Start oven. After 4 minutes, ask an adult to help you remove the cover. Arrange slashed hot dogs atop hot bean mixture. Micro-cook, covered, on high for 4 to 5 minutes more or till hot dogs have curled, as shown. Makes 4 servings.

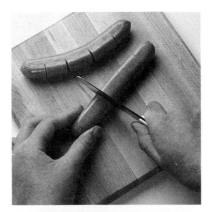

To slash the hot dogs, use a table knife to make four crosswise slits in each, as shown. Be sure you only cut partway through. With the slits, the hot dogs will curl easily.

When you arrange the slashed hot dogs on the hot bean mixture, give them room to move, because the heat makes them curl, as shown.

Twisty Macaroni and Cheese

EQUIPMENT

large saucepan	rubber scraper
measuring cups	1½-quart casserole
hot pads	sharp knife
colander	cutting board
bottle opener	

Make your macaroni and cheese with a twist—twisty noodles, that is. These curly noodles are called corkscrew macaroni because they look like the kind of openers adults use to remove corks from wine bottles.

Macaroni takes too long to cook in the microwave oven so cook it on the range, but be careful with the hot element, hot water, and steam.

1 cup corkscrew *or* elbow macaroni

● On the range top, in a large saucepan cook the macaroni following the package directions. Ask an adult to help you drain the macaroni in a colander.

1 5-ounce jar American cheese spread
¼ cup milk

● Use a bottle opener to open the jar of cheese spread. Use a rubber scraper to push the cheese spread into a 1½-quart nonmetal casserole. Stir in the milk.

● Cover with the lid. Place in the microwave oven; set on full or high (100%) power. Set the timer for 2 minutes. Start oven. After 2 minutes, stir with the rubber scraper till the mixture is smooth. If the cheese is not melted, micro-cook, covered, on high for 10 seconds to 1 minute more.

● Stir the drained macaroni into the mixture. Micro-cook, covered, on high for 3 minutes. After 3 minutes, if the mixture is not hot, micro-cook, covered, on high for 15 seconds to 1 minute more. Ask an adult to help you remove the cover.

If you can't eat all the macaroni and cheese at once, cover and chill it for later. When you get hungry, put about ⅔ cup onto a nonmetal plate. Micro-cook, uncovered, on high for 45 seconds to 1 minute or till hot.

1 medium tomato (if you like)

● If you want to use the tomato, ask an adult to help you use a sharp knife and a cutting board to chop it. Throw away seeds. Sprinkle tomato atop macaroni mixture. Micro-cook, uncovered, on high for 30 seconds to 1 minute more or till hot. Makes 4 servings.

Bread	+ **Spread**	+ **Meat**	+ **Cheese**
2 slices white bread	Mayonnaise *or* salad dressing	4 slices bacon	1 slice American cheese
2 slices whole wheat bread	Sweet pickle relish	¼ cup canned deviled ham *or* beef *or* chicken spread	1 slice Swiss cheese
2 slices rye bread	Catsup	¼ cup canned tuna *or* salmon	1 slice mozza- rella cheese
1 hamburger bun, split	Butter *or* margarine, softened	1 slice bologna *or* luncheon meat	1 slice cheddar cheese
1 hot dog bun, split	Prepared mustard	6 slices very thinly sliced cooked turkey, chicken, ham, corned beef, *or* pastrami	1 slice Monterey Jack cheese

Sandwiches, sandwiches, and more sandwiches. Play chef and mix and match breads, spreads, meats, cheeses, and vegetables to come up with your own creations. Put part of the fixings onto each slice of bread and micro-cook. Slap the slices together and you're ready for the best part—eating.

Mix and Matchwiches

+ Vegetable	Equipment
4 thin cucumber slices	**toaster**
2 tomato slices	**table knife**
4 dill pickle slices	**kitchen scissors *or* can opener**
Lettuce leaves	**2 plates**
½ cup alfalfa sprouts	**paper towels**
	strainer *and* fork
	hot pads

● Toast the bread slices or bun halves, if you like. Use a table knife to spread one side of each bread slice or bun half with the spreads that you want.

● For meat, open any packages or cans. If using bacon, place slices on a nonmetal plate between *white* paper towels. Micro-cook on high for 2 minutes and 30 seconds to 3 minutes or till crisp; crumble. Or, drain and stir canned meat or fish with a fork. Throw away any skin and bones in fish.

● Put your choice of meat onto one bread slice or bun half. Put a cheese slice onto the other.

● Put the open sandwich halves onto a nonmetal plate. Do not cover. Place in the microwave oven; set on full or high (100%) power. Set the timer for 30 seconds. Start oven. After 30 seconds, if halves are not warm, micro-cook, uncovered, on high for 10 to 30 seconds more.

● Put 1 or 2 vegetable choices on top of meat and top with the other sandwich half, cheese side down. Makes 1 serving.

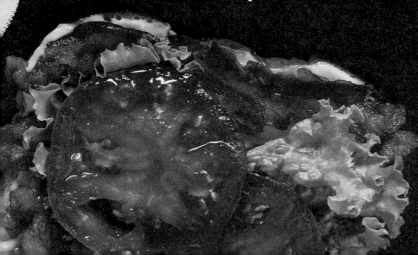

Tiny Tuna Pockets

EQUIPMENT

can opener	shredder
strainer	waxed paper
medium mixing bowl	measuring cups
small mixing bowl	measuring spoon
container	kitchen scissors
fork	small spoon
sharp knife	white paper towel
cutting board	large plate

"Mmmmmm" was all we heard when our six young tasters bit into this juicy sandwich. We think you'll agree with them.

---

1 8-ounce can crushed pineapple
1 3½-ounce can tuna

● Use a can opener to open the cans of pineapple and tuna. Drain the pineapple in a strainer over a medium mixing bowl. Put the pineapple into a small mixing bowl. Save the juice in a tightly covered container in the refrigerator for another use. Drain the tuna. Add the tuna to the pineapple. Use a fork to break the tuna into small pieces.

---

1 head cabbage

● Ask an adult to help you use a sharp knife and a cutting board to cut a wedge from the cabbage. Use a shredder and waxed paper to shred the cabbage. Measure to see that you have ½ cup. Add to the pineapple and tuna. Save the rest of the cabbage for another use.

---

2 slices American cheese
1 tablespoon mayonnaise or salad dressing

● Use your hands to tear the cheese into small pieces. Stir the cheese and mayonnaise into the tuna mixture.

---

4 small pita bread rounds

● Use kitchen scissors to cut each pita bread in half crosswise. Spoon about ¼ cup of the tuna filling into each half.

● Put a white paper towel onto a large nonmetal plate. Arrange the filled pita halves in a circle on top. Do not cover. Place in the microwave oven; set on full or high (100%) power. Set the timer for 1 minute and 15 seconds. Start oven. After 1 minute and 15 seconds, if the mixture is not warm, micro-cook, uncovered, on high for 15 to 30 seconds more. Makes 4 servings.

To heat just 1 serving, cut *1* small pita bread round in half crosswise. Spoon about ¼ cup of the tuna filling into *each* half. Micro-cook the 2 halves, uncovered, on high for 35 to 45 seconds or till hot. Store the remaining filling in a tightly covered container in the refrigerator.

Micro-cook the chilled leftover filling in 2 pita bread halves, uncovered, on high for 45 to 50 seconds or till hot.

Velvety Cheese Soup

EQUIPMENT

2 table knives	can opener
2-quart casserole	cutting board
hot pads	ruler
measuring cups	ladle
rubber scraper	4 soup bowls

Turn cheese chunks and crackers into boats floating on a steamy, creamy cheese sea.

We discovered it was easier to cut the cheese into chunks if we dipped the table knife into cold water before cutting.

3 tablespoons butter *or* margarine

● Put the butter or margarine into a 2-quart nonmetal casserole. Do not cover. Place in the microwave oven; set on full or high (100%) power. Set the timer for 30 seconds. Start oven. After 30 seconds, if not melted, micro-cook, uncovered, on high for 15 to 30 seconds more.

¼ cup all-purpose flour
1 10¾-ounce can condensed chicken broth
2 cups milk

● Use a rubber scraper to stir the flour into the melted butter. Use a can opener to open the can of chicken broth. Stir the broth and milk into the flour mixture.

Micro-cook, uncovered, on high for 6 to 7 minutes or till slightly thickened and bubbly. *After every minute,* stir from the outside to the center. Micro-cook, uncovered, on high for 1 minute more.

1 8-ounce package cheese spread

● On a cutting board use a table knife and ruler to cut the cheese into ½-inch cubes. Set aside *8* of the cubes. Stir the rest of the cubes into the hot mixture.

Micro-cook, uncovered, on high for 1 to 2 minutes or till the cheese is melted, stirring once. Ladle the soup into 4 nonmetal soup bowls.

Put two crackers atop the soup in each bowl. Place a cheese cube onto each cracker, as shown. You can eat the soup right away or melt the chunks of cheese in the microwave oven first.

8 saltine crackers, rich round crackers, *or* melba toast rounds

● Put *2* crackers on the soup in *each* bowl. Place a cheese cube onto each cracker, as shown. If you want to melt the cheese, micro-cook each bowl of soup, uncovered, on high for 30 seconds or till melted. Makes 4 servings.

Microwave Heating Times for Lunch Foods

How long is it until lunch time? Not very long at all if you use the microwave oven to heat your favorite packaged foods. You can have a steaming bowl of soup, a sizzling hot dog, or a plate of saucy spaghetti in a snap if you follow these easy heating directions.

Soup: Pour one 10- to 11-ounce can of *condensed soup* into a 4-cup liquid measuring cup. Stir in 1 can of *water*. Cover with waxed paper. Micro-cook on high for 2 minutes and 30 seconds to 3 minutes and 30 seconds or till hot.

Pour one 7- to 8-ounce can of *semi-condensed soup* into a nonmetal bowl. Add ½ can of *water*. Cover. Micro-cook for 2 minutes and 15 seconds to 2 minutes and 45 seconds or till hot.

Sandwich: Put 1 frozen *sandwich* onto a *white* paper towel on a nonmetal plate. Micro-cook, uncovered, on high for 1 minute to 1 minute and 30 seconds or till sandwich is hot. (Large sandwiches may take 2 minutes to 2 minutes and 30 seconds.)

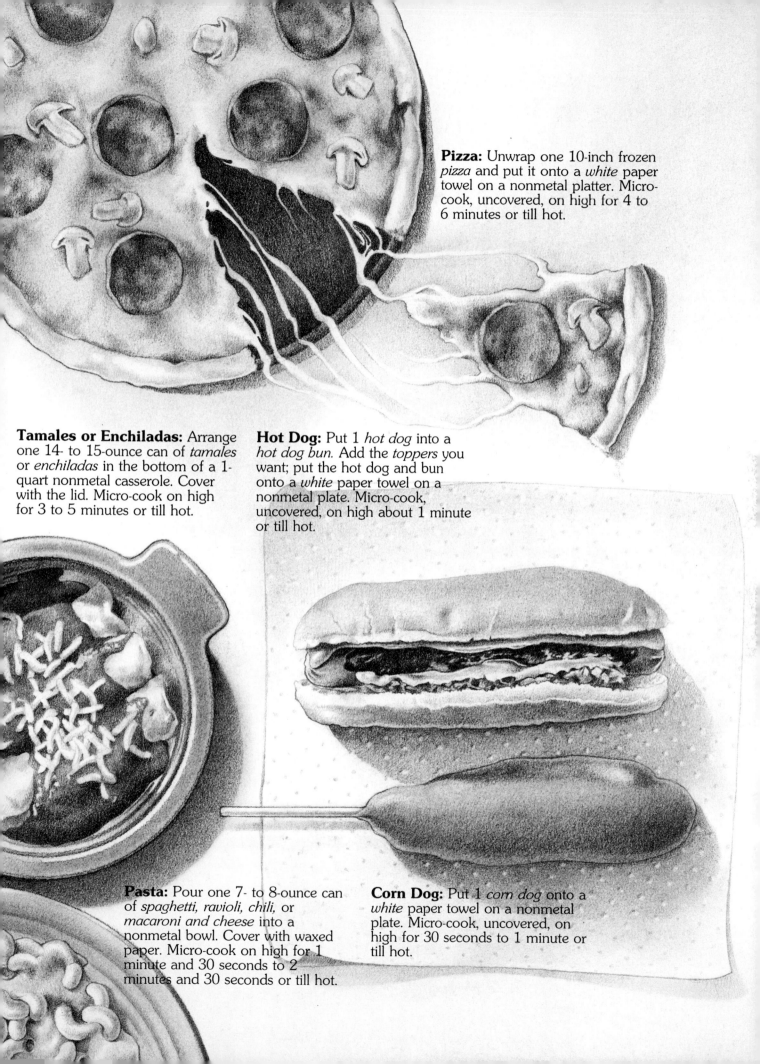

Pizza: Unwrap one 10-inch frozen *pizza* and put it onto a *white* paper towel on a nonmetal platter. Micro-cook, uncovered, on high for 4 to 6 minutes or till hot.

Tamales or Enchiladas: Arrange one 14- to 15-ounce can of *tamales* or *enchiladas* in the bottom of a 1-quart nonmetal casserole. Cover with the lid. Micro-cook on high for 3 to 5 minutes or till hot.

Hot Dog: Put 1 *hot dog* into a *hot dog bun.* Add the *toppers* you want; put the hot dog and bun onto a *white* paper towel on a nonmetal plate. Micro-cook, uncovered, on high about 1 minute or till hot.

Pasta: Pour one 7- to 8-ounce can of *spaghetti, ravioli, chili,* or *macaroni and cheese* into a nonmetal bowl. Cover with waxed paper. Micro-cook on high for 1 minute and 30 seconds to 2 minutes and 30 seconds or till hot.

Corn Dog: Put 1 *corn dog* onto a *white* paper towel on a nonmetal plate. Micro-cook, uncovered, on high for 30 seconds to 1 minute or till hot.

Snowy Meat Loaf Peaks

EQUIPMENT

table knife	12x7½x2-inch
large mixing bowl	baking dish
fork	waxed paper
measuring cups	hot pads
measuring spoons	pancake turner
plastic bag	dinner plate
rolling pin	1-quart casserole
wooden spoon	narrow metal
½- or ¾-cup funnel	spatula

Shaping these mountains is a lot like making sand castles with a bucket, only you use meat. To help the ground beef come out of the funnel when you turn it upside down, run a table knife or metal spatula around the edge to loosen it. And if you don't have a funnel, don't worry; you can form peaks with your hands.

---

1 egg
¼ cup catsup-style hamburger relish
2 tablespoons milk
½ teaspoon Italian seasoning

● Use a table knife to crack the egg; open and pour into a large mixing bowl. Stir with a fork. Stir in the catsup-style hamburger relish, milk, and Italian seasoning.

---

7 saltine crackers

● Put crackers into a plastic bag; close. Use a rolling pin to finely crush. Stir the crushed crackers into egg mixture.

---

1 pound lean ground beef

● Use your hands to crumble ground beef into egg mixture. Use a wooden spoon to mix. For *each* peak, spoon *one-fourth* of the meat mixture into a ½- or ¾-cup funnel; press down. Turn upside down into a 12x7½x2-inch nonmetal baking dish. Cover with waxed paper.

● Place the dish in the microwave oven; set on full or high (100%) power. Set the timer for 4 minutes. Start oven. After 4 minutes, use hot pads to turn the dish halfway around. *Carefully* remove the cover. Micro-cook on high for 3 to 5 minutes more or till no pink remains. Use a pancake turner to transfer the peaks to a nonmetal plate.

Packaged instant mashed potatoes (enough for 4 servings)
Pepper, snipped parsley, *or* paprika

● In a 1-quart nonmetal casserole or saucepan make mashed potatoes, following package directions. Use a narrow metal spatula to spread the potatoes over tops of peaks, as shown. Micro-cook, uncovered, on high for 1 to 2 minutes or till hot. Sprinkle with pepper, parsley, or paprika. Serves 4.

Make the mashed potato "snow" in the microwave oven or on the range top, using package directions.

After you've coated the peaks with the snow, sprinkle parsley "moss" or pepper "rocks" on top.

Hot Tamale Bake

EQUIPMENT

measuring cup	table knife
plastic bag	ruler
rolling pin	1½-quart casserole
sharp knife	large spoon
cutting board	hot pads
can opener	

When you want to make dinner for yourself and a group of friends or your family, we have just the recipe for you. This easy dish tastes a little like chili, and a little like tacos. It is sure to please anyone lucky enough to get a bite! You'll have plenty to share with five other people.

2 cups corn chips
1 medium onion

● Put the corn chips into a plastic bag. Close the bag. Use a rolling pin or your hands to break chips. Set aside. Ask an adult to help you use a sharp knife and cutting board to chop the onion. Set the chopped onion aside.

1 15-ounce can tamales
1 15-ounce can chili
**   without beans**

● Use a can opener to open the cans of tamales and chili. Remove and throw away the paper wrapper from each tamale. On the cutting board use a table knife and a ruler to slice the tamales crosswise into ½-inch-thick slices. Lay *half* of the slices over the bottom of a 1½-quart nonmetal casserole. Spoon *half* of the chili over the tamale slices. Sprinkle *half* of the chopped onion and *half* of the broken chips on top.

6 slices American cheese

● Arrange *3* of the cheese slices over the corn chips. Layer the remaining tamale slices, chili, and onion on top. Save the remaining chips and cheese. Cover the casserole with the lid.

● Place the casserole in the microwave oven; set on full or high (100%) power. Set the timer for 4 minutes. Start oven. After 4 minutes, use hot pads to turn the dish halfway around. Micro-cook on high for 4 minutes more. If the mixture is not hot all the way through, micro-cook for 1 to 2 minutes more.

● Ask an adult to help you *carefully* remove the cover. Arrange the remaining cheese slices on top of the hot mixture. Sprinkle with the remaining corn chips. Micro-cook, uncovered, on high for 1 to 2 minutes more or till the cheese is melted. Makes 6 servings.

Freckled Chicken

EQUIPMENT

measuring spoons	pastry brush
table knife	rack *or* 2 saucers
measuring cup	12x7½x2-inch
small spoon	baking dish
hot pads	waxed paper
paper towel	

Anyone with freckles will know why we named this bird "Freckled Chicken." The sesame seed sticks to the honey-mustard glaze just like those freckles dot your nose.

3 tablespoons honey
2 tablespoons prepared mustard
1 tablespoon butter *or* margarine
2 teaspoons Worcestershire sauce

● Put the honey, mustard, butter or margarine, and Worcestershire sauce into a 1-cup liquid measuring cup. Use a small spoon to stir. Do not cover. Place in the microwave oven; set on full or high (100%) power. Set the timer for 1 minute. Start oven. After 1 minute, stir the mixture again.

8 chicken drumsticks
2 tablespoons sesame seed

● Rinse the chicken drumsticks and pat dry with a paper towel. Use a pastry brush to brush the chicken with the honey mixture. Sprinkle the chicken with sesame seed.

Place a nonmetal rack or 2 upside-down saucers in a 12x7½x2-inch nonmetal baking dish. Arrange the drumsticks on top of rack or saucers, with the meatiest parts toward the outside, as shown. Cover the dish with waxed paper.

Place a nonmetal rack or two upside-down saucers in the baking dish. Then, arrange the chicken on top of the rack or saucers, as shown. That way, the fat that cooks out of the chicken will drain off. For even cooking, arrange the drumsticks so the meatiest parts are toward the outside.

● Micro-cook on high for 5 minutes. After 5 minutes, use hot pads to turn the dish halfway around. Micro-cook for 5 to 7 minutes more or till no pink color remains. Before serving, drizzle any remaining honey mixture over the cooked chicken. Makes 4 servings.

Cheesy Quiches

EQUIPMENT

waxed paper	ruler
4 10-ounce custard cups	mixing bowl
	fork
cutting board	kitchen scissors
table knife	measuring cup
rolling pin	hot pads

Have you ever had pie for supper, instead of for dessert? These quiches (KEESH-es) are like little pies, but they aren't sweet. The crust is made of biscuits and the filling is made of eggs and cheese.

Butter *or* margarine
1 package (6) refrigerated biscuits

● Grease four 10-ounce custard cups with butter or margarine. Open the can of biscuits following the package directions. On a cutting board use a table knife to cut *2* of the biscuits into 8 pie-shaped wedges (16 wedges). Set the wedges aside.

Use your hands or a rolling pin to flatten the remaining biscuits into 4- to 5-inch-wide circles. Place *1* flattened biscuit into *each* custard cup, pressing the biscuit against the bottom and up the sides of the custard cup.

---

3 eggs
1 8-ounce package (2 cups) shredded cheddar cheese
Paprika *or* chili powder (if you like)

● Use the table knife to crack each egg; open and pour each one into a mixing bowl. Stir the eggs with a fork. Use kitchen scissors to open the package of cheese. Stir the cheese into the eggs. Scoop *one-fourth* of the egg mixture (about ⅓ cup) into *each* custard cup. Arrange *4* of the biscuit wedges on top of the egg mixture in *each* custard cup. Sprinkle the biscuit wedges with paprika or chili powder, if you like. Do not cover. Arrange the custard cups in a circle in the microwave oven.

● Set the microwave oven on full or high (100%) power. Set the timer for 2 minutes. Start oven. After 2 minutes, use hot pads to rearrange the custard cups. To rearrange, move each cup to a new spot in the circle. Micro-cook, uncovered, on high for 2 minutes more. If the edges are not set, micro-cook on high for 1 to 2 minutes more. Let the quiches stand for 5 minutes before serving. Serves 4.

When the quiches have finished cooking, the cheesy filling will be firm around the edges, but it will still jiggle slightly at the center.

Piled-High Peppers

EQUIPMENT

measuring cups	8x8x2-inch
hot pads	baking dish
wooden spoon	waxed paper
clear plastic wrap	2 plastic bags
sharp knife	meat mallet
cutting board	measuring spoons
small spoon	

Carve your own edible boats from green peppers or tomatoes to hold this nutty, fruity rice dish to eat with meats, chicken, or fish.

You can make just the rice filling to eat without the vegetable boats, too. Simply stir the peanuts, raisins, and cinnamon into the cooked rice in the 2-cup liquid measuring cup. Do not cover. Micro-cook on high for 30 to 60 seconds or till hot.

½ cup orange juice

● Pour the orange juice into a 2-cup liquid measuring cup. Do not cover. Place in the microwave oven; set on full or high (100%) power. Set the timer for 45 seconds. Start oven. After 45 seconds, if juice is not bubbly, micro-cook, uncovered, on high for 15 seconds more.

½ cup Minute Rice

● Use a wooden spoon to stir the rice into the juice. Cover with clear plastic wrap. Let stand for 5 minutes while you prepare the green pepper or tomato.

---

2 small green peppers or 4 medium tomatoes
Salt

● Ask an adult to help you use a sharp knife and a cutting board to cut the green pepper in half from top to bottom. Throw away the stem, membrane, and seeds, as shown. (*Or,* cut the tops off of the tomatoes. Use a small spoon to scoop out centers, leaving ¼-inch-thick shells.) Sprinkle the insides with salt. Put the *pepper halves,* cut side up, into an 8x8x2-inch nonmetal baking dish. Cover with waxed paper. Micro-cook the peppers on high for 4 minutes. (Do not micro-cook the tomatoes.)

After an adult has helped you cut the green pepper in half, pull out the seeds with your fingers. Then, grasp the light-colored membrane and pull it out, as shown.

¼ cup peanuts
2 tablespoons raisins
⅛ teaspoon ground cinnamon

● Put the peanuts into a plastic bag inside a second plastic bag. Close the bags. Set on the cutting board. Use a meat mallet to chop. Stir the chopped peanuts, raisins, and cinnamon into the cooked rice. Scoop *one-fourth* of the rice mixture (about ⅓ cup) into *each* pepper half or tomato.

● Put filled vegetables into the baking dish. Do not cover. Micro-cook peppers on high for 3 minutes or tomatoes for 2 minutes. Makes 4 servings.

No-Tie Shoestrings

EQUIPMENT

2 table knives	cutting board
measuring cups	kitchen scissors
hot pads	10x6x2-inch baking
rubber scraper	dish
measuring spoons	waxed paper

Leave your shoelaces in your shoes, because we're talking about French-fried shoestring potatoes. Zac said they looked a lot like his brother's shoestrings, which are always untied. But all the kids agreed—these don't taste like shoestrings! You smother these skinny fries in a cheesy sauce, so you'll need a fork to eat them.

2 tablespoons butter *or* margarine

● Put the butter or margarine into a 4-cup liquid measuring cup. Do not cover. Place in the microwave oven; set on full or high (100%) power. Set the timer for 15 seconds. Start oven. After 15 seconds, if the butter or margarine is not melted, micro-cook, uncovered, on high for 15 to 30 seconds more.

2 tablespoons all-purpose flour
1⅓ cups milk

● Use a rubber scraper to stir the flour into the melted butter. Stir in the milk. Do not cover. Micro-cook on high for 3 minutes. *After every minute,* stir from the outside to the center. After 3 minutes, if the mixture is not thickened and bubbly, micro-cook, uncovered, on high for 1 to 2 minutes more.

4 ounces cheese spread

● On a cutting board use a table knife to cut the cheese into small cubes. Stir into the hot sauce. Micro-cook, uncovered, on high about 1 minute or till the cheese is melted.

1 20-ounce package frozen French-fried crinkle-cut shoestring potatoes

● Use kitchen scissors to open the package of potatoes. Spread the potatoes in a 10x6x2-inch nonmetal baking dish. Pour the cheese sauce over the potatoes. Cover with waxed paper. Micro-cook on high for 5 minutes. Use hot pads to turn the dish halfway around. Micro-cook on high for 5 minutes more. If the potatoes are not hot, micro-cook on high for 1 to 2 minutes more. Makes 6 servings.

Bunny Bundles

EQUIPMENT

measuring cup	sharp knife
measuring spoons	cutting board
2-quart casserole	ruler
hot pads	tongs
wooden spoon	fork
vegetable peeler	slotted spoon

Any respectable rabbit would jump at an invitation to your house when you serve these colorful bundles. And you'll love them too—the green onions tie up tasty vegetables to go with your supper. Just be sure the green onions are completely soaked in the broth, to make them easier to tie.

---

2 cups water
1 tablespoon instant
   chicken bouillon
   granules
½ teaspoon minced dried
   onion

● Put the water, bouillon granules, and onion into a 2-quart nonmetal casserole. Cover with the lid. Place in the microwave oven; set on full or high (100%) power. Set the timer for 6 minutes. Start oven. After 6 minutes, use hot pads to remove the casserole from oven. Ask an adult to help you *carefully* remove the lid. Stir the mixture with a wooden spoon till the bouillon granules are dissolved.

---

1 medium carrot
1 stalk celery *or* broccoli
8 whole green beans
4 green onions

● Meanwhile, use a vegetable peeler to peel the carrot. Ask an adult to help you use a sharp knife and a cutting board to cut the tops and bottoms from carrot and celery; cut in half crosswise, then in half lengthwise to make 4 sticks of each. (*Or,* if using broccoli, cut into four pieces about the same size as the carrot sticks.) Use your hands to break ends off each green bean. Pull off the strings.

   Trim white ends from each onion, leaving 8-inch-long green onion tops. Use tongs to dip the whole green onion tops into the hot broth for 10 seconds. Set the broth aside.

Hot broth makes the green onion limp, so you can tie it around the vegetables. (Be careful when you dip the green onion tops into the broth because the steam can burn.) To tie, put four vegetable sticks crosswise onto each onion top. Lift the onion ends up around the vegetables. Tuck one onion end under the other and pull gently, as shown.

● Arrange *4* vegetables together—*1* carrot stick, *1* piece of celery or broccoli, and *2* green beans—across *each* green onion top. Tie the onion top around the vegetables, as shown. Repeat with the remaining vegetables and onion tops.

● Put the vegetable bundles into the hot broth. Cover with the lid. Micro-cook the bundles on high for 8 to 10 minutes or till the vegetables are tender when poked with a fork. Ask an adult to help you *carefully* remove the cover. Use a slotted spoon to remove the bundles from broth. Makes 4 servings.

Double-Corn Scallop

EQUIPMENT

plastic bag	rubber scraper
rolling pin	measuring cup
table knife	8x1½-inch round
medium mixing	baking dish
bowl	small mixing bowl
2 forks	hot pads
can opener	measuring spoon
colander	

During one of our taste panels, we decided to make this dish extra corny by adding whole kernel corn. See if you like it as much as we did.

---

18 rich round cheese crackers

● Put the crackers into a plastic bag. Close the bag. Use a rolling pin or your hands to crush the crackers.

---

1 egg
1 8¾-ounce can whole kernel corn
1 8½-ounce can cream-style corn
1 7½-ounce can semi-condensed cream of mushroom soup

● Use a table knife to crack the egg; open and pour it into a medium mixing bowl. Stir with a fork. Use a can opener to open both cans of corn and the can of soup. Drain the whole kernel corn in a colander. Use a rubber scraper to push both kinds of corn and the soup into the bowl with the egg. Stir in ½ *cup* of the crushed crackers. Scrape the mixture into an 8x1½-inch round nonmetal baking dish. Set the baking dish aside while you make the topping.

---

1 tablespoon butter *or* margarine
1 teaspoon dried parsley flakes

● For the topping, put the butter or margarine into a small nonmetal mixing bowl. Do not cover. Place in the microwave oven; set on full or high (100%) power. Set the timer for 15 seconds. Start oven. If the butter is not melted, micro-cook on high for 15 seconds more. Use a fork to stir in the remaining crushed crackers and the parsley flakes.

● Sprinkle the topping on the corn mixture. Micro-cook, uncovered, on high for 8 to 10 minutes or till hot. Let stand for 5 minutes. Makes 4 servings.

Fancy Hat Rolls

EQUIPMENT
pastry brush
plate
table knife

4 purchased whole wheat dinner rolls
Milk
Dried dillseed, dried dillweed, poppy seed, rolled oats, caraway seed, sesame seed, toasted wheat germ, grated Parmesan cheese, *or* **coarse salt**
Butter *or* **margarine**

● Use a pastry brush to spread the milk on top of the rolls. Sprinkle each roll with a different topper, as shown. Put the rolls onto a nonmetal plate. Do not cover. Place in the microwave oven; set on full or high (100%) power. Set the timer for 20 seconds. Start oven. After 20 seconds, if the rolls are not barely warm to the touch, micro-cook, uncovered, on high for 5 to 10 seconds more. Serve warm with butter. Makes 4.

Here's a special bread for dinner. Each person can choose a topper or hat. The milk makes the topper stick to the rolls. Ryan, the eight-year-old who made this recipe in our Test Kitchen, declared, "I like the Parmesan rolls the best!"

Microwave Heating Times for Supper Foods

When you want to make supper simple, try heating some of these easy foods in a microwave oven. You can make your own menu by combining the roll or French-fried potatoes, your favorite green vegetable, and the chicken or fish. For dessert, turn to page 93.

Fried Chicken: Put 2 frozen *fried chicken pieces* onto a *white* paper towel on a nonmetal plate, with the meatiest parts of each piece toward the outside. Cover with another *white* paper towel. Micro-cook on high for 3 to 4 minutes or till hot.

Dinner Rolls: Put 2 *dinner rolls* onto a *white* paper towel on a nonmetal plate. Micro-cook, uncovered, on high for 20 seconds (if room temperature) or 30 seconds (if frozen).

Corn on the Cob: Rinse 1 unpeeled ear of *corn*. (If peeled, wrap in waxed paper.) Put ear onto a nonmetal plate. Micro-cook, uncovered, on high for 3 minutes. Let stand for 5 minutes. When the ear is cool enough to handle, peel off husks and silk or waxed paper. Rinse under warm water.

Fish Sticks: Put 3 frozen *breaded fish sticks* onto a *white* paper towel on a nonmetal plate. Cover with another *white* paper towel. Micro-cook on high for 1 minute and 30 seconds to 2 minutes or till hot.

Frozen Vegetables: Open one 10-ounce package of frozen *asparagus, lima beans, broccoli, brussels sprouts,* or *mixed vegetables.* Put the vegetables into a 1½-quart nonmetal casserole. Add 2 tablespoons *water.* Cover with the lid. Micro-cook on high for 8 to 10 minutes or till tender, stirring vegetables or turning dish halfway around *after 4 minutes.*

Micro-cook one 9- or 10-ounce package of frozen *green beans, cauliflower, corn, peas, spinach,* or *zucchini,* following the directions above, *but* micro-cook on high for 6 to 8 minutes, stirring vegetables or turning the dish halfway around *after 3 minutes.*

Frozen Dinner: Remove the tray from the carton of one 9- to 16-ounce frozen *3-part dinner* in a paper tray. (Do not use foil trays.) Use a fork to prick holes in the plastic film. Micro-cook on high for 7 to 8 minutes, turning the tray halfway around *after 4 minutes.*

French-Fried Potatoes: Put 1 cup of frozen *French-fried potatoes* onto a *white* paper towel on a nonmetal plate. Cover with another *white* paper towel. Micro-cook on high for 2 to 3 minutes or till hot.

Chinese Egg Drop Soup

EQUIPMENT

measuring spoon	table knife
1½-quart casserole	small bowl
can opener	fork
rubber scraper	ladle
measuring cup	4 soup bowls
hot pads	

1 tablespoon cornstarch
2 14½-ounce cans chicken broth
½ cup frozen mixed Japanese-style *or* Oriental-style vegetables

● Put the cornstarch into a 1½-quart nonmetal casserole. Use a can opener to open the cans of chicken broth. Using a rubber scraper to stir, slowly pour the broth into the casserole with the cornstarch. Stir in the frozen vegetables. Cover the casserole with the lid.

● Place in the microwave oven; set on full or high (100%) power. Set the timer for 4 minutes. Start oven. After 4 minutes, ask an adult to help you use hot pads to *carefully* remove the cover. Use the rubber scraper to stir the soup from the bottom to the top. Return the cover. Micro-cook on high about 4 minutes more or till bubbly. Stir again. Micro-cook, covered, on high for 2 minutes more.

1 egg

● Meanwhile, use a table knife to crack the egg; open and pour it into a small bowl. Stir with a fork. Pour the egg into the hot soup; stir once. Serve at once. To serve, use a ladle to spoon the soup into 4 soup bowls. Makes 4 servings.

Watch closely as you stir in the beaten egg. It will begin to cook as soon as it touches the hot soup. In fact, that's how Chinese Egg Drop Soup earned its name. Because you stir in the egg, it cooks in shreds or drops. Be careful not to stir too much though, or the egg will get completely mixed into the soup and the drops will disappear.

5

3

2

1

Mexican Beef Tostadas

EQUIPMENT

sharp knife	long-handled
cutting board	spoon
kitchen scissors *or*	container for fat
shredder	measuring cups
1-quart casserole	measuring spoons
hot pads	small spoon
rubber scraper	

With one spicy recipe, you can make two Mexican dishes—tostadas and tacos. The zesty filling is the same for both. The only difference is the shell you use. For tostadas, pile the filling on top of a flat corn tortilla shell. For tacos, spoon the filling into the center of a bent corn tortilla shell.

---

1 medium tomato
¼ of a medium head lettuce
1 4-ounce package (1 cup) shredded cheddar cheese *or* 4 ounces cheddar cheese

● Ask an adult to help you use a sharp knife and a cutting board to chop the tomato and slice the lettuce into strips. Use kitchen scissors to open the package of cheese or use a shredder to shred a 4-ounce block of cheese. Set aside.

¾ pound ground beef

● Use your hands to crumble the ground beef into a 1-quart nonmetal casserole. Cover with the lid. Place in the microwave oven; set on full or high (100%) power. Set the timer for 2 minutes. Start oven. After 2 minutes, ask an adult to help you use hot pads to *carefully* remove the cover. Use a rubber scraper to stir the beef from the outside to the center. Return the cover.

● Micro-cook on high for 1 to 2 minutes more or till no pink color remains. Ask an adult to help you use a long-handled spoon to spoon off the fat.

¼ cup chili sauce
2 teaspoons minced dried onion
⅛ teaspoon garlic salt

● Put chili sauce, onion, and garlic salt into a 1-cup liquid measuring cup. Stir with a small spoon. Stir sauce mixture into cooked meat. Micro-cook, covered, on high about 30 seconds or till hot.

---

8 tostada shells
Taco sauce

● Spoon the meat mixture onto the tostada shells (1). Top with lettuce (2), tomato (3), cheese (4), and taco sauce (5). Makes 4 servings.

Mexican Beef Tacos: Follow the recipe above, *but* use 8 *taco shells* instead of tostada shells. Spoon the meat mixture into taco shells. Top with lettuce, tomato, cheese, and taco sauce.

Italian Lasagna

EQUIPMENT

large saucepan	table knife
colander	medium mixing
10x6x2-inch baking	bowl
dish	fork
hot pads	measuring cups
rubber scraper	can opener
long-handled spoon	kitchen scissors
container for fat	waxed paper
paper towel	foil

6 lasagna noodles

● On the range top, in a large saucepan cook the noodles following the package directions. Ask an adult to help you drain the noodles in a colander.

¾ pound bulk Italian sausage *or* ground beef

● Use your hands to crumble the meat into a 10x6x2-inch nonmetal baking dish. Do not cover. Place in the microwave oven; set on full or high (100%) power. Set the timer for 3 minutes. Start oven. *After 2 minutes,* use a rubber scraper to stir meat from outside to center. *After 3 minutes,* if meat is not all brown, micro-cook, uncovered, on high for 30 seconds to 2 minutes more. Ask an adult to help you to spoon off fat, as shown. Put meat onto a paper towel.

1 egg
1 cup cream-style cottage cheese *or* ricotta cheese
¼ cup grated Parmesan *or* Romano cheese

● Use a table knife to crack the egg; open and pour into a medium mixing bowl. Stir with a fork. Stir in the *undrained* cottage cheese or ricotta cheese and Parmesan or Romano cheese. Stir in the cooked meat.

1 8-ounce can pizza sauce
1 6-ounce package sliced mozzarella cheese

● Open the can of pizza sauce and package of mozzarella cheese. In baking dish lay *half* of the noodles lengthwise. Spread *half* of the meat mixture on top. Lay *half* of mozzarella cheese on meat. Pour *half* of sauce over all. Layer remaining noodles, meat, cheese, and sauce on top, as shown. Cover with waxed paper. Micro-cook on high for 8 to 9 minutes or till hot all the way through. Cover with foil; let stand for 10 minutes. Remove foil and waxed paper. Cut the lasagna into squares to serve. Makes 6 servings.

We liked spicy Italian sausage in our lasagna, but if you want a milder flavor, you might use the ground beef instead.

Use a long-handled spoon to push the meat to one side of the dish. Tip the dish so the fat runs to the other side. Use the spoon to carefully remove the hot fat, as shown. Put the fat into a metal or glass container.

Putting the lasagna together is easy. Simply layer half of the noodles, half of the meat mixture, half of the mozzarella cheese, and half of the pizza sauce in the baking dish, then repeat the layers, as shown.

Chicken Cacciatore

EQUIPMENT

large saucepan	waxed paper
measuring cups	hot pads
can opener	cutting board
rubber scraper	table knife
measuring spoons	colander
10x6x2-inch baking dish	

Cacciatore (pronounced kotch-a-TOR-e) is an Italian word that means cooked with tomatoes and herbs. This chicken dish has not only tomato sauce and herbs, but also cheese and pasta. Chicken Cacciatore is a fancy food and, with our recipe, it's easy, too.

---

4 ounces tiny shell *or* corkscrew macaroni (1⅓ cups)

● On the range top, in a large saucepan cook the macaroni following package directions. When the macaroni is cooked, let stand, covered, in the saucepan while you micro-cook the chicken and sauce.

---

1 8-ounce can tomato sauce
½ teaspoon sugar
¼ teaspoon dried basil, crushed
¼ teaspoon dried marjoram, crushed

● Use a can opener to open the can of tomato sauce. Pour the tomato sauce into a 2-cup liquid measuring cup. Use a rubber scraper to scrape out the can and to stir in the sugar, basil, and marjoram.

---

2 whole medium chicken breasts, skinned, halved lengthwise, and boned (1 pound)

● Arrange the chicken breast halves in a 10x6x2-inch nonmetal baking dish. Pour the tomato sauce mixture over the chicken. Cover with waxed paper. Place in the microwave oven; set on full or high (100%) power. Set the timer for 6 minutes. Start oven. After 6 minutes, if parts of the chicken are still pink, micro-cook, covered, on high for 1 minute to 2 minutes and 30 seconds more or till no pink color remains.

---

1 1½-ounce slice mozzarella cheese
Snipped parsley

● On a cutting board use a table knife to cut the cheese slice into 4 equal pieces. Lay *one* piece of cheese on top of *each* chicken breast half. Micro-cook, uncovered, on high for 1 minute.

　　Ask an adult to help you drain the cooked macaroni in a colander. Spoon about ⅓ *cup* of the macaroni onto each of 4 dinner plates. Arrange the chicken and sauce on top. Sprinkle with the parsley. Makes 4 servings.

Round-Up Submarine

EQUIPMENT
2 table knives
kitchen scissors
white paper towel

You can rustle up a ranch-style hot beef sandwich about as well as any cowhand. This sandwich is so big, it looks like a submarine. In fact, if you haven't worked up a stampeding appetite, you may want to cut it in half to share with another cowpoke.

1 **6-inch-long French-style roll**
   Prepared mustard, catsup, or horseradish sauce
   Mayonnaise or salad dressing

● Use a table knife to cut the roll in half lengthwise. Spread the bottom half with mustard, catsup, or horseradish sauce. Spread the top half with mayonnaise or salad dressing.

1 **3-ounce package very thinly sliced smoked roast beef, turkey, or pastrami**
2 **thin tomato slices**

● Use kitchen scissors to open the package of meat. Put the meat onto the bottom half of the bun. Add the tomato slices and cover with top half of bun, mayonnaise-side down.

● Wrap the sandwich in a *white* paper towel. Place in the microwave oven; set on full or high (100%) power. Set the timer for 30 seconds. Start oven. After 30 seconds, if the sandwich is not warm, micro-cook on high for 10 to 30 seconds more. Makes 1 serving.

Belt-Busting Burgers

EQUIPMENT

ruler	pancake turner
8x8x2-inch baking dish	2 table knives
	sharp knife
waxed paper	cutting board
hot pads	

Our kid taste-testers thought these hamburgers were some of the best they had ever eaten. You can make these burgers just the way you like them, because we've given you lots of choices of things to put on the burger or on the bun.

1 pound lean ground beef

● Use your hands to shape the meat into four 4-inch-wide patties. Put the patties into an 8x8x2-inch nonmetal baking dish. Cover with waxed paper.

Place in the microwave oven; set on full or high (100%) power. Set the timer for 3 minutes. Start oven. After 3 minutes, use a pancake turner to turn the patties over. Micro-cook, covered, on high for 3 minutes more. Let stand, covered, for 1 to 2 minutes to finish cooking, while you prepare the buns.

4 hamburger buns, split
Mayonnaise *or* salad dressing
Prepared mustard *or* catsup

● Use a table knife to spread the bottom halves of buns with mayonnaise or salad dressing. Spread mustard or catsup onto top halves of buns.

1 medium tomato
Lettuce leaves *or* alfalfa sprouts
Dill pickle slices *or* sweet pickle relish

● Ask an adult to help you use a sharp knife and cutting board to slice the tomato. Put a lettuce leaf or alfalfa sprouts and tomato slices onto bottom halves of buns.

Use the pancake turner to remove the cooked burgers from dish; place on top of tomato slices. Top with dill pickle slices or pickle relish and the tops of the buns. Makes 4 servings.

Cheeseburgers: Follow the recipe above, *but* put 1 slice *American cheese* onto each cooked meat patty after cooking. Let the cheese melt during the 1 to 2 minutes standing time. If not melted after the standing time, micro-cook, uncovered, for 20 to 30 seconds.

Really Chili

EQUIPMENT
1½-quart casserole	can opener
hot pads	measuring cup
rubber scraper	measuring spoons
long-handled spoon	ladle
container for fat	4 soup bowls

You can make this chili really hot or really mild. For hot chili, use hot-style taco sauce and the full teaspoon of chili powder. Use regular taco sauce and the smaller amount of chili powder for a milder version of the chili.

1 pound ground beef

● Use your hands to crumble the ground beef into a 1½-quart nonmetal casserole. Cover with the lid. Place in the microwave oven; set on full or high (100%) power. Set the timer for 3 minutes. Start oven.

● After 3 minutes, ask an adult to help you use hot pads to *carefully* remove the lid. Use a rubber scraper to stir from the outside to the center. Return the lid and micro-cook the meat about 2 minutes more or till no pink color remains. Ask an adult to help you use a long-handled spoon to spoon off the fat.

1 15-ounce can red kidney beans
1 5½-ounce can (⅔ cup) tomato juice
⅓ cup taco sauce
½ to 1 teaspoon chili powder
¼ teaspoon onion salt *or* garlic salt

● Use a can opener to open the can of beans and the can of tomato juice, if necessary. Stir the *undrained* beans, tomato juice, taco sauce, chili powder, and onion or garlic salt into the cooked beef. Cover with the lid. Micro-cook on high for 5 minutes. Ask an adult to help you *carefully* remove the lid. Stir once; return the lid and micro-cook for 2 to 3 minutes more or till hot.

Fix chili dogs with leftover chili, following the recipe on the opposite page. Or, simply reheat a bowlful of leftover chili. To reheat 1 cup, micro-cook the chilled chili, covered, on high for 2 to 3 minutes or till hot (5 to 6 minutes for frozen chili), stirring once.

Tortilla chips (if you like)
Shredded cheddar *or* Monterey Jack cheese (if you like)
Dairy sour cream (if you like)

● Use a ladle to spoon the chili into 4 soup bowls. If you like, top each bowl of chili with some tortilla chips, cheese, and sour cream. Makes 4 servings.

Home-Run Hot Dogs

EQUIPMENT

table knife	white paper
cutting board	towel *or* plate
3 small spoons	hot pads

4 **hot dogs**
4 **hot dog buns**
2 **slices American cheese**
   (if you like)
   Sweet pickle relish
   Prepared mustard
   Catsup

● Put *1* hot dog into *each* bun. If you are using cheese, use a table knife and a cutting board to cut *each* cheese slice into *4* strips. Put *2* strips into *each* bun, overlapping ends. Use spoons to spread relish, mustard, and catsup on top of each hot dog.

● Put hot dogs onto a *white* paper towel or a nonmetal plate. Do not cover. Place in the microwave oven; set on full or high (100%) power. Set the timer for 2 minutes and 30 seconds. Start oven. After 2 minutes and 30 seconds, if not hot, micro-cook, uncovered, on high for 10 to 30 seconds more. Serves 4.

Chili Dogs: Follow the recipe above, *but* don't use relish, mustard, or catsup. Tear the cheese into pieces and set aside. Use a can opener to open one 7½-ounce can *chili without beans.*

   Spread about *2 tablespoons* of the chili on top of *each* hot dog. (Chill leftover chili for another use.) Sprinkle hot dogs with cheese. Micro-cook, uncovered, on high for 2 minutes and 30 seconds to 3 minutes or till hot.

Hot dogs make a big hit anywhere, whether you're at the ball park or at home watching the game on television. Make them with "the works" (cheese, pickle relish, mustard, and catsup), or with chili and cheese.

To prepare just one hot dog, micro-cook it, uncovered, on high for 40 to 50 seconds or till hot. Micro-cook two hot dogs for 1 minute to 1 minute and 15 seconds.

Rub-a-Dub Tub Chicken

EQUIPMENT

measuring cups   paper towel
plastic bag   pastry brush
rolling pin   rack *or* 2 saucers
measuring spoons 12x7½x2-inch
table knife   baking dish
small bowl   waxed paper
hot pads

This seasoned, coated chicken was a favorite with our young friends. "Delicious," they said, and they licked their fingers between every juicy bite.

---

2 cups crisp rice cereal
¼ cup toasted wheat germ
½ teaspoon Italian seasoning
½ teaspoon paprika
¼ teaspoon salt

● Put the cereal into a plastic bag. Close bag. Use a rolling pin or your hands to crush. Add the wheat germ, seasoning, paprika, and salt to the crushed cereal in the plastic bag; shake to mix.

---

2 tablespoons butter *or* margarine

● Put the butter or margarine into a small nonmetal bowl. Do not cover. Place in the microwave oven; set on full or high (100%) power. Set the timer for 15 seconds. Start oven. If the butter is not melted after 15 seconds, micro-cook on high for 15 to 30 seconds more.

---

1 2½- to 3-pound broiler-fryer chicken, cut up

● Rinse the chicken pieces and pat dry with a paper towel. Use a pastry brush to brush chicken pieces with the melted butter or margarine. Put chicken, 1 or 2 pieces at a time, into the plastic bag with the crushed cereal mixture. Shake to coat the chicken with the mixture. Remove the chicken from the bag.

● Place a nonmetal rack or 2 upside-down saucers in a 12x7½x2-inch nonmetal baking dish. Arrange chicken on top, with the meatiest parts toward the outside. Sprinkle any remaining crushed cereal mixture on top of the chicken. Cover with waxed paper.
   Micro-cook on high for 8 minutes. After 8 minutes, use hot pads to turn the dish halfway around. Micro-cook on high for 4 minutes more. After 4 minutes, if parts of the chicken are still pink, micro-cook, covered, on high for 1 to 2 minutes more or till no pink color remains. Makes 6 servings.

Chic'n-Lic'n Nuggets

EQUIPMENT

measuring spoons	rolling pin
9-inch pie plate	slotted spoon
waxed paper	cutting board
hot pads	container for liquid
2 table knives	wooden spoon
small mixing bowl	measuring cup
fork	small bowl
plastic bag	

Eat these juicy chunks of chicken with your fingers or a fork, or spear them with toothpicks. Choose from three sauces—barbecue, sweet-sour, or mustard-mayonnaise. Heat the sauce in the microwave oven and dip the nuggets in.

---

2 whole medium chicken breasts, skinned, halved lengthwise, and boned (1 pound)
1 tablespoon water

● Put chicken and 1 tablespoon water into a 9-inch nonmetal pie plate. Cover with waxed paper. Place in microwave oven; set on full or high (100%) power. Set timer for 3 minutes. Start oven. Use hot pads to turn dish halfway around. Micro-cook for 2 minutes more. If parts of chicken are still pink, micro-cook about 1 minute more or till no pink remains. Let stand 5 minutes.

---

1 egg
1 tablespoon water
16 rich round crackers

● Use a table knife to crack the egg; open and pour into a small mixing bowl. Add 1 tablespoon water; stir with a fork.
　Put the crackers into a plastic bag; close bag. Use a rolling pin to finely crush, as shown.

Put the crackers into a plastic bag. Close the bag and lay it on a flat surface. Use a rolling pin to finely crush the crackers, as shown.

● When chicken is cool enough to handle, use a slotted spoon to transfer to a cutting board. Ask an adult to help you pour liquid out of pie plate into container. Cut chicken into bite-size chunks. Dip chunks into egg mixture, then put into bag with crushed crackers. Close bag; shake to coat the chicken with the crushed crackers, as shown.

---

2 tablespoons butter *or* margarine

● Put butter into pie plate. Micro-cook 15 seconds. If not melted, micro-cook 15 to 30 seconds more. Add coated chicken. Micro-cook, uncovered, for 1 minute. Use a wooden spoon to stir. Micro-cook for 1 to 2 minutes more or till hot.

Put the chicken pieces into the plastic bag with the crushed crackers. Shake the bag, as shown, to coat the chicken with the crushed crackers.

½ cup bottled barbecue sauce, sweet-sour sauce, *or* mustard-mayonnaise sandwich and salad sauce

● Put sauce into a small nonmetal bowl. Micro-cook, uncovered, on high for 1 minute or till hot. To serve, dip the chicken into sauce. Makes 4 servings.

Egg 'n' Muffin Stack

EQUIPMENT

toaster	hot pads
table knife	fork
10-ounce custard cup	plate

1 English muffin, split	● Toast the English muffin halves in a toaster. Set aside.
1 teaspoon butter _or_ margarine	● Put the butter or margarine into a 10-ounce nonmetal custard cup. Do not cover. Place in the microwave oven; set on full or high (100%) power. Set the timer for 15 seconds. Start oven.
1 egg	● After 15 seconds, use a table knife to crack the egg; open and pour it into the custard cup with the melted butter. Use a fork to stir the yolk and white together. Micro-cook the egg and butter, uncovered, on high for 45 seconds.
1 slice boiled ham	● Put the bottom half of the muffin onto a nonmetal plate. Top with the ham, folding or tearing it to fit the muffin half.
1 slice American cheese	● Use hot pads to slide the egg out of the custard cup onto the ham. Put the cheese on top of the egg. Micro-cook, uncovered, on high for 15 to 20 seconds or till the cheese starts to melt. Put the top half of the muffin onto the cheese. Makes 1 serving.

You build your breakfast stack like this: Put the ham on the muffin, the egg on the ham, the cheese on the egg, and the muffin on the cheese. Then micro-cook it and taste why our young cooks said, "Yummm....This is better than the ones you get in a restaurant!"

Crazy Pizza Wheels

EQUIPMENT

measuring cup	can opener
measuring spoon	paper towel
2 table knives	vegetable peeler
white paper towel	shredder *or*
large plate	sharp knife
cutting board	hot pads

These pizzas are a little crazy because they have a muffin or a tostada crust instead of the regular crust. You'll find these crusts are the right size to hold in your hands. And we've given you lots of ideas for toppers, so you can make your pizza the way you like it best.

½ cup pizza sauce *or* spaghetti sauce
2 English muffins, split, *or* 4 tostada shells

● Use a measuring spoon to put about *2 tablespoons* of the sauce onto *each* English muffin half or tostada shell. Use a table knife to spread. Place the muffin halves onto a *white* paper towel on a large nonmetal plate. Place the tostada shells onto a large nonmetal plate.

1½ ounces sliced pepperoni, salami, fully cooked ham, *or* 1 hot dog

● On a cutting board, use a table knife to cut the pepperoni, salami, or ham into small pieces, or the hot dog into thin slices. Set aside.

Sliced mushrooms (canned), sliced pitted green olives, carrot, *or* green onion

● Use a can opener to open any cans or jars. Drain the mushrooms and olives on a paper towel. Ask an adult to help you use a vegetable peeler and a shredder to peel and shred the carrot or a sharp knife to chop the green onion.

Arrange the meat and as much of the vegetable toppers as you like on top of the sauce on the muffin halves or tostada shells. Do not cover.

● Place the plate in the microwave oven; set on full or high (100%) power. Set the timer for 1 minute. Start oven. After 1 minute, use hot pads to turn the plate halfway around. Micro-cook, uncovered, on high for 1 minute more.

½ cup shredded mozzarella cheese (2 ounces)

● Sprinkle the pizzas with the cheese. Micro-cook, uncovered, on high for 30 seconds to 1 minute more or till cheese is melted. Makes 4 servings.

Be-My-Valentine Pie

EQUIPMENT

measuring cup	hot pads
rubber scraper	large spoon

1 cup water
1 3-ounce package
  strawberry-flavored
  gelatin

● Measure the water in a 4-cup liquid measuring cup. Use a rubber scraper to stir in the gelatin. Do not cover. Place in the microwave oven; set on full or high (100%) power. Set timer for 1 minute and 30 seconds. Start oven. After 1 minute and 30 seconds, if the gelatin is not dissolved, micro-cook, uncovered, on high for 30 seconds more.

1 pint vanilla ice cream
  (2 cups)

● Add the vanilla ice cream to the hot gelatin mixture, one spoonful at a time, stirring till the ice cream is melted. Chill the mixture in the refrigerator for 25 to 30 minutes, stirring twice during chilling. The mixture should mound when you drop it from a spoon.

1 chocolate-flavored crumb
  pie shell
  Pressurized dessert
  topping (if you like)
  Chocolate-flavored
  sprinkles *or* small
  chocolate candies
  (if you like)

● Pour the chilled ice cream mixture into the pie shell. Chill in the refrigerator about 4 hours or till the ice cream mixture does not jiggle if tilted slightly. If you like, decorate the pie with dessert topping and chocolate sprinkles or candies. Makes 6 to 8 servings.

Surprise a friend on Valentine's Day with this special pie. The filling is a fluffy pink strawberry mixture that firms up in the refrigerator.

After the pie chills, decorate it with dessert topping and chocolate sprinkles or candies. Look for small chocolate hearts in grocery or candy stores just before Valentine's Day. Or, use chocolate pieces, stars, or kisses.

Gingerbread Faces

EQUIPMENT

measuring cups
measuring spoons
small mixing bowl
fork
rubber scraper
medium mixing
  bowl
wooden spoon
2 table knives
small bowl

clear plastic wrap
rolling pin
ruler
4-inch round
  cookie cutter
platter
hot pads
pancake turner
cooling rack

Jamie had fun making and decorating our big, quick-cooking cookies, and he liked using his hands to mix the dough. He says, "It's pretty easy to tell when these cookies are done, because the tops start to look dry."

1¾ **cups all-purpose flour**
½ **teaspoon ground ginger**
¼ **teaspoon baking soda**
¼ **teaspoon ground cinnamon**
¼ **cup shortening**
¼ **cup sugar**
1 **egg**
¼ **cup molasses**

● Put flour, ginger, baking soda, and cinnamon into a small mixing bowl. Use a fork to stir till mixed. Set aside.

Put shortening and sugar into a medium mixing bowl; stir with a wooden spoon. Use a table knife to crack the egg; open and pour egg into a small bowl. Add the egg to shortening mixture. Add molasses. Stir till well mixed. (Mixture will not be smooth.)

● Add *one-third* of the flour mixture to molasses mixture. Stir with the wooden spoon. Add *half* of the remaining flour mixture and stir. Add remaining flour mixture; stir. If dough gets too stiff to stir, use your hands to mix. Shape it into a ball; wrap it in clear plastic wrap. Chill dough in the refrigerator for 2 hours.

● Unwrap the chilled dough on a lightly floured surface. Use a rolling pin to roll the dough into a 10-inch circle. Use a 4-inch round cookie cutter to cut the dough into eight circles.

Put *four* of the circles onto a nonmetal platter. Do not cover. Place in the microwave oven; set on full or high (100%) power. Set the timer for 1 minute and 30 seconds. Start oven. After 1 minute and 30 seconds, turn the platter halfway around. Micro-cook for 1 minute to 1 minute and 30 seconds more or till cookies look dry on top.

---

1 **can vanilla, chocolate,** *or*
  lemon frosting
  Assorted decorations
  (see tip, opposite)

● Let cookies cool on plate for 2 minutes. Use a pancake turner to transfer to a cooling rack. Micro-cook four more cookies as directed above. Reroll any scraps; micro-cook. Let cool completely before frosting with a table knife. Decorate the cookies. Makes 8 cookies.

Wish your parents happy Mother's or Father's Day with cookies made to look just like them! Here are some decorating suggestions:

HAIR: corn flakes, crushed shredded wheat biscuits, coconut, chocolate-flavored sprinkles, shoestring licorice, small oval mints, multicolored decorative candies

EYES: peanut butter-flavored, butterscotch, or chocolate pieces; peanuts; candied cherries; raisins; caramel pinwheels; fruit-flavored or white circle candies; small round candies; jelly candies, gumdrops; round toasted oat cereal

NOSE: sliced almonds, cashews, dates, candy corn, candied pineapple, tiny marshmallows, milk chocolate stars or kisses, candy-coated milk chocolate pieces

MOUTH: fruit-flavored circle candies, red cinnamon candies, gumdrops, shoestring licorice

FRECKLES: sesame seed, small multicolored decorative candies

EYEBROWS and LASHES: cashews, shoestring licorice, chocolate-flavored sprinkles

BOW TIE: shoestring licorice, candied pineapple

CHEEKS: gumdrops, red cinnamon candies, candied cherries, fruit leather

Swirl Cupcakes

EQUIPMENT

measuring cups	microwave
measuring spoons	muffin pan
2 mixing bowls	12 paper bake
2 forks	cups
table knife	small spoon
small bowl	hot pads
shredder	toothpick
waxed paper	cooling rack
sharp knife	can opener
cutting board	narrow metal
juicer	spatula

Say "Happy Birthday" to someone with these strawberry-lemon cupcakes. They're so pretty because you marble pink and yellow batters together. Be careful to stir the batters only once, so the yellow and pink just barely swirl.

---

1 cup all-purpose flour
¾ cup sugar
1½ teaspoons baking powder
Dash salt
½ cup milk
¼ cup cooking oil
1 egg

● Put the flour, sugar, baking powder, and salt into a mixing bowl. Use a fork to stir. Stir in the milk and cooking oil. Use a table knife to crack the egg; open and pour it into a small bowl. Add egg to flour mixture. Stir till well mixed.

---

2 teaspoons strawberry
preserves
Few drops red food
coloring
1 lemon
Few drops yellow food
coloring

● Put *1 cup* of the batter into a second mixing bowl. Stir in the strawberry preserves and red coloring. Set aside. Ask an adult to help you use a shredder to finely shred the lemon peel and a sharp knife to halve the lemon. Use a juicer to juice lemon. Measure ¼ *teaspoon* peel and *1 tablespoon* juice. Use a fork to stir peel, juice, and yellow coloring into the first bowl of batter.

● Line a microwave muffin pan with bake cups (1). Spoon *1 tablespoon* of *each* batter into *each* cup (2, 3). Stir once with a spoon to swirl (4). Do not cover. Place pan in microwave oven; set on full or high (100%) power. Set timer for 1 minute and 30 seconds. Start oven. *After 1 minute,* turn pan. After 1 minute and 30 seconds, insert a toothpick near center. If the pick comes out clean, the cupcakes are done. If batter sticks to pick, micro-cook, uncovered, for 15 to 30 seconds more.

You can micro-cook the cupcakes in six 6-ounce custard cups instead of a microwave muffin pan. Arrange the cups in a circle in the microwave oven. After 1 minute, move each cup to a new spot in the circle so the cupcakes cook evenly.

---

1 can lemon *or* strawberry
frosting
Small multicolored
decorative candies

● When done, ask an adult to help you *carefully* transfer cupcakes to cooling rack. Use the remaining batter to make 6 more cupcakes. When the cupcakes are cool, use a narrow metal spatula to spread them with lemon or strawberry frosting. Sprinkle decorative candies on top. Makes 12 cupcakes.

Caramel Apple People

EQUIPMENT

8 wooden sticks	rubber scraper
kitchen scissors	waxed paper
measuring cups	small spoon
measuring spoon	8 plastic foam
hot pads	drinking cups

8 medium apples
**1 14-ounce package
vanilla and chocolate
caramels**
2 tablespoons water

● Push a wooden stick into the stem end of each apple. Set aside. Use kitchen scissors to open the package of caramels. Unwrap the caramels and put into a 4-cup liquid measuring cup. Add the water. Do not cover. Place in the microwave oven; set on full or high (100%) power. Set timer for 2 minutes. Start oven. After 2 minutes, use a rubber scraper to stir. Micro-cook, uncovered, on high for 30 seconds to 1 minute and 30 seconds more or till melted. Stir till smooth.

**½ cup sunflower nuts,
miniature semisweet
chocolate pieces, *or*
Grape Nuts cereal**

● Put sunflower nuts, chocolate pieces, or cereal onto waxed paper; set them aside. Dip each apple into the hot caramel, using a spoon to spread the mixture evenly over apple. Hold the apple over the caramel to allow the excess to drip off into the measuring cup. Dip the bottom into sunflower nuts, chocolate pieces, or cereal. Turn plastic foam cups upside down and push sticks through the bottoms. (*Or,* place apples upside down on waxed paper.)

When Cindy made her Caramel Apple People, she came up with the idea of pushing the sticks into the bottoms of upside-down plastic foam cups instead of setting the caramel apples upside down on waxed paper.

The cups held the apples right side up, making them easier for Cindy to decorate. We thought her method was such a good idea that we included it in our recipe.

**Assorted candies and nuts
(see tip, opposite)**

● While the caramel coating is still warm, use candies and nuts to decorate the apples, making them look like Halloween goblins or like people. Makes 8 caramel apples.

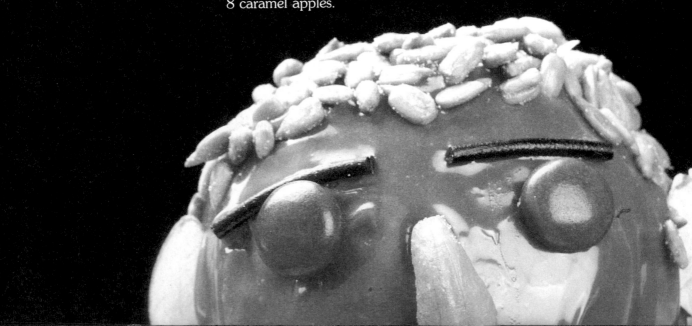

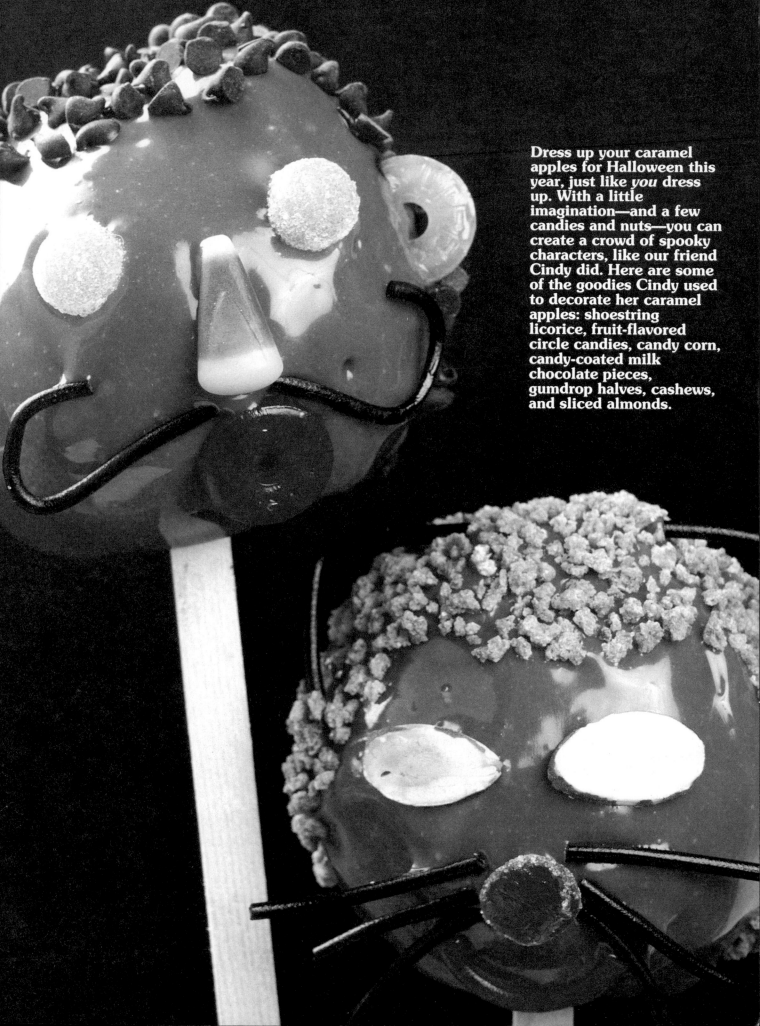

Dress up your caramel apples for Halloween this year, just like *you* dress up. With a little imagination—and a few candies and nuts—you can create a crowd of spooky characters, like our friend Cindy did. Here are some of the goodies Cindy used to decorate her caramel apples: shoestring licorice, fruit-flavored circle candies, candy corn, candy-coated milk chocolate pieces, gumdrop halves, cashews, and sliced almonds.

Candy-Stripe Parfaits

EQUIPMENT

measuring cups	8 parfait glasses
1-quart casserole	small mixing bowl
3 rubber scrapers	measuring spoon
hot pads	

These pretty red and green parfaits can add festive color to your holidays, as a dessert, a salad, or a snack. Make them by layering two flavors of gelatin in parfait glasses.

To keep the red and green layers from running together, be sure the lime gelatin is set, but still jiggles a little, before you add the cherry gelatin.

1 3-ounce package lime-flavored gelatin
1 cup water

● Put lime-flavored gelatin and 1 cup water into a 1-quart nonmetal casserole. Use a rubber scraper to stir. Do not cover. Place in the microwave oven; set on full or high (100%) power. Set the timer for 1 minute and 30 seconds. Start oven. After 1 minute and 30 seconds, stir well. If the gelatin is not dissolved (liquid should be clear), micro-cook, uncovered, on high for 30 seconds more.

1 3-ounce package cherry-flavored gelatin
1 cup water

● Put the cherry-flavored gelatin and 1 cup water into a 4-cup liquid measuring cup. Stir well. Micro-cook, uncovered, on high for 1 minute and 30 seconds to 2 minutes or till dissolved.

2 cups cold water

● Stir *1 cup* of the cold water into *each* flavor of gelatin. Carefully pour ¼ *cup* of the lime gelatin into *each* parfait glass. Chill in the refrigerator about 1 hour or till gelatin is thick, but jiggles slightly if tilted. Meanwhile, let the cherry gelatin stand at room temperature.

● Carefully pour ¼ *cup* of the cherry gelatin on top of *each* thick lime gelatin layer. Chill for several hours or till the gelatin doesn't jiggle when tilted.

½ cup plain *or* fruit-flavored yogurt
½ cup frozen whipped dessert topping, thawed
¼ cup coconut
8 maraschino cherries

● Put the yogurt, dessert topping, and coconut into a small mixing bowl. Gently stir with a rubber scraper till mixed. Top *each* cherry gelatin layer with about *2 tablespoons* of the yogurt mixture. Place *one* cherry on top of the yogurt mixture on *each* serving. Makes 8 servings.

Butterscotch Pudding

EQUIPMENT

table knife	clear plastic wrap
small bowl	measuring spoons
slotted spoon	rubber scraper
measuring cups	hot pads
fork	4 dessert glasses

This pudding can be the start of three deliciously different desserts. Try spooning the chilled pudding into dessert glasses by itself, or make it into parfaits, or fill tart shells using the recipes on opposite page.

1 egg

● Use a table knife to crack the egg; open and pour it into a small bowl. Lift out the unbroken yolk with your hand or a slotted spoon. Place the yolk into a 1-cup liquid measuring cup. Stir with a fork. Set aside. (Cover the egg white in the small bowl with clear plastic wrap; save in refrigerator for another use.)

½ cup packed brown sugar
2 tablespoons cornstarch
¼ teaspoon salt
1⅔ cups milk

● Put the brown sugar, cornstarch, and salt into a 4-cup liquid measuring cup. Stir with a rubber scraper till well mixed. Pour in a little milk. Stir till smooth. Slowly pour in the rest of the milk. Stir till smooth. Do not cover.

● Place in the microwave oven; set on full or high (100%) power. Set the timer for 2 minutes. Start oven. After 2 minutes, stir from the outside to the center. Micro-cook, uncovered, on high for 2 to 3 minutes more or till thickened and bubbly, stirring *after every minute.*

● Use a measuring cup to spoon *some* of the hot milk mixture into the beaten egg yolk. Stir the hot egg mixture with the fork till well mixed. Pour the egg mixture into the rest of the milk mixture in the 4-cup liquid measuring cup. Stir till well mixed. Do not cover.

3 tablespoons butter
** *or* margarine**
1 teaspoon vanilla

● Micro-cook, uncovered, on high for 30 seconds or till mixture is bubbly. Add the butter or margarine and vanilla. Stir just till butter is completely melted and mixed in. Cover the top of the pudding with clear plastic wrap, using your fingers to gently press the wrap onto the surface of the pudding. Chill for 1 hour.

● Pour the pudding into 4 dessert glasses. Chill in the refrigerator till serving time. Makes 4 servings.

Butterscotch Parfaits

EQUIPMENT

plastic bag	measuring spoons
rolling pin	4 parfait glasses

Layer pudding and crumbled cookies in tall dessert glasses and you'll have an elegant dessert. If you like, you can make your favorite flavor of pudding from a packaged pudding mix, instead of our Butterscotch Pudding.

Butterscotch Pudding (see recipe opposite) *or* **one package 4-serving-size butterscotch pudding mix**	● Prepare Butterscotch Pudding. (*Or,* prepare the packaged pudding mix, following the package directions.) Cover and chill the pudding.
4 chocolate wafers, soft macaroons, *or* **small chocolate chip cookies**	● Put the cookies or macaroons into a plastic bag. Close the bag. Use a rolling pin or your hands to crumble or crush the cookies.
	● Spoon about *2 rounded tablespoons* of the pudding into *each* parfait glass. Sprinkle with *some* of the crushed cookies. Repeat layers; then top with the remaining pudding. Chill till serving time. Makes 4 servings.

Butterscotch Tarts

EQUIPMENT

plastic bag	fork
rolling pin	4 6-ounce
table knife	custard cups
small mixing bowl	

For these tarts, our young cooks crushed chocolate wafers and mixed them with melted butter to prepare four mini chocolate crusts. Then they added Butterscotch Pudding.

On taste panel, Amy ate her tart and was ready for seconds even before we could ask how everyone else liked theirs. The other kids ate more slowly, but they liked the tarts as much as Amy did.

Butterscotch Pudding (see recipe opposite) *or* **one package 4-serving-size butterscotch pudding mix**	● Prepare Butterscotch Pudding. (*Or,* prepare the packaged pudding mix, following the package directions.) Cover and chill the pudding.
18 chocolate wafers	● Put wafers into a plastic bag. Close bag. Use a rolling pin to crush the wafers. Set aside.
¼ cup butter *or* **margarine**	● Put butter or margarine into a small nonmetal mixing bowl. Do not cover. Place in the microwave oven; set on full or high (100%) power. Set timer for 30 seconds. Start oven. If butter is not melted after 30 seconds, micro-cook for 10 to 15 seconds more.
	● Use a fork to stir crushed wafers into melted butter. Put *one-fourth* of the mixture into *each* custard cup. Use your hands to press evenly onto the bottom and sides. Chill for 1 hour. Pour *one-fourth* of the pudding into *each* tart shell. Chill till serving time. Makes 4 servings.

You can dip lots of other foods into this fondue, too. Try orange sections, peach slices, pitted dark sweet cherries, bite-size doughnut pieces, or large marshmallows. Spear the food with fondue forks, cocktail forks, or dinner forks, then dip into the fondue. Use another fork to eat the dipped food.

Chocolate Fondue

Dip chunks of fruit and small pieces of cake into this thick, fudgy fondue for a delicious dessert.

The fondue may get too stiff to eat easily as it cools. Warm the fondue by micro-cooking, uncovered, on high for 30 seconds. Stir till smooth.

EQUIPMENT

sharp knife	punch-type
cutting board	can opener
pastry brush	hot pads
kitchen scissors	rubber scraper
medium mixing	measuring spoon
bowl	forks

Whole fresh strawberries; seedless grapes; or apples, pears, pineapple, or bananas
Angel cake, or chocolate or plain pound cake
Lemon juice

● Choose the fruits or cake you want to use and prepare them for dipping. Ask an adult to help you use a sharp knife and cutting board to core the apples and pears and peel the pineapple. Peel the bananas. Ask an adult to help you cut the fruit and the cake into bite-size pieces. Brush cut edges of apples, pears, and bananas with lemon juice to keep the fruit from turning brown. Set aside.

1 11½-ounce package (2 cups) milk chocolate pieces
1 5⅓-ounce can (⅔ cup) evaporated milk

● Use kitchen scissors to open the package of chocolate pieces. Put the chocolate pieces into a medium nonmetal mixing bowl. Use a punch-type can opener to open the can of evaporated milk. Pour the evaporated milk into the bowl with the chocolate pieces. Do not cover.

Store any leftover fondue in a tightly covered container in the refrigerator. To reheat the chilled leftover fondue, put it into a nonmetal mixing bowl. Micro-cook, uncovered, on high for 30 seconds to 1 minute and 30 seconds or till warm enough for dipping.

¼ teaspoon almond extract (if you like)

● Place in the microwave oven; set on full or high (100%) power. Set the timer for 1 minute and 30 seconds. Start oven. After 1 minute and 30 seconds, if the chocolate pieces are not soft enough to stir smooth with a rubber scraper, micro-cook, uncovered, on high for 30 seconds more. Add the almond extract, if you like. Stir till smooth. Spear pieces of fruit and cake with a fork and dip them into fondue, as shown. Makes 1¾ cups.

Candied Pear Crisp

EQUIPMENT

can opener	rubber scraper
strainer	9-inch pie plate
medium mixing bowl	table knife
container	small mixing bowl
measuring spoons	fork
hot pads	measuring cups
	ice cream scoop

You mix caramels with fruit to make this gooey dessert. Even though "pear" is in the name, you can use canned apples instead and you'll find the dessert tastes a lot like caramel apples.

---

1 29-ounce can pear slices *or* one 20-ounce can sliced apples

● Open the can of pears or apples. Put a strainer onto a medium nonmetal mixing bowl. Pour in pears or apples so the juice drains into bowl. Set fruit aside. Pour juice into a container. Return *2 tablespoons* of the juice to mixing bowl. Store remaining juice, tightly covered, in refrigerator for another use.

---

8 vanilla caramels

● Unwrap caramels; put caramels into bowl with juice. Do not cover. Place in the microwave oven; set on full or high (100%) power. Set timer for 1 minute and 30 seconds. Start oven. Use a rubber scraper to stir till smooth. If caramels are not soft enough to stir smooth, micro-cook, uncovered, on high for 15 to 30 seconds more.

---

1 teaspoon lemon juice

● Add drained fruit and the lemon juice to the bowl. Stir till fruit is coated with caramel. Use the rubber scraper to scrape fruit and caramel mixture into a 9-inch nonmetal pie plate. Set aside.

---

3 tablespoons butter *or* margarine
2 tablespoons brown sugar
½ cup quick-cooking rolled oats
¼ cup all-purpose flour
¼ teaspoon ground cinnamon

● Put butter or margarine into a small nonmetal mixing bowl. Micro-cook, uncovered, on high for 30 to 60 seconds or till melted. Use a fork to stir in the brown sugar. Add oats, flour, and cinnamon. Stir till crumbly. Sprinkle over mixture in pie plate. Do not cover.

Vanilla ice cream (if you like)

● Micro-cook on high for 4 minutes. Turn dish halfway around. Micro-cook on high for 3 to 4 minutes more or till hot. Serve warm with vanilla ice cream, if you like. Makes 4 servings.

Cinnamon Baked Apples

EQUIPMENT

sharp knife	hot pads
cutting board	measuring cup
vegetable peeler	measuring spoon
9-inch pie plate	rubber scraper
table knife	small spoon
small mixing bowl	

4 medium apples

● Place 1 whole apple, stem end up, on a cutting board. Ask an adult to help you use a sharp knife to core the apple. (Push the knife into the top of the apple close to the stem. Cut all the way around the stem. Turn the apple upside down and repeat. Use your fingers to pull the core out of the apple.) Repeat with the remaining apples.

Use a vegetable peeler to cut the peel from the top third of each apple. Arrange the apples, peeled end up, in a 9-inch nonmetal pie plate. Set aside.

1 tablespoon butter *or* margarine
¼ cup raisins
1 tablespoon chopped walnuts
1 tablespoon brown sugar
1 tablespoon red cinnamon candies

● Put the butter or margarine into a small nonmetal mixing bowl. Do not cover. Place in the microwave oven; set on full or high (100%) power. Set the timer for 15 seconds. Start oven. If the butter is not melted after 15 seconds, micro-cook, uncovered, on high for 15 seconds more. Add the raisins, chopped walnuts, brown sugar, and cinnamon candies to the melted butter. Use a rubber scraper to stir till well mixed.

● Put about *1 tablespoon* of the raisin mixture into the center of *each* apple in the pie plate, as shown. Use your fingers to push the mixture down. Spoon in any remaining mixture and press down.

Do not cover. Micro-cook on high for 3 minutes. Use hot pads to turn the dish halfway around. Micro-cook, uncovered, on high for 3 minutes more or till apples are tender. Let the apples stand, uncovered, for 15 minutes before serving. Makes 4 servings.

As the apples cook, the brown sugar and cinnamon candies make a spicy red syrup. Spoon a little of the syrup over each apple before eating.

Store any leftover baked apples in a tightly covered container in the refrigerator. To reheat a chilled baked apple, place it in a nonmetal dish. Micro-cook, uncovered, on high for 45 seconds to 1 minute or till hot all the way through.

Spoon the raisin mixture into the hollowed center of each apple, as shown. Then use your fingers to push the mixture down into the apple.

Doughnut Sundaes

EQUIPMENT

table knife	kitchen scissors
measuring spoons	*or* can opener
measuring cups	hot pads
rubber scraper	small plates
	ice cream scoop

**Raspberry Topping,
  Pineapple Topping, *or*
  Hot Fudge Topping
Cake doughnuts
Ice cream**

● Prepare one of the toppings below. For each serving, put one doughnut onto a small plate. Top with a scoop of ice cream and some of the warm topping.

**1 tablespoon cornstarch
¼ teaspoon ground
    cinnamon
¼ cup orange juice
1 10-ounce package frozen
    red raspberries, thawed**

● **Raspberry Topping:** Put cornstarch and cinnamon into a 4-cup liquid measuring cup. Add orange juice. Use a rubber scraper to stir. Open and stir in raspberries. Do not cover. Place in the microwave oven; set on full or high (100%) power. Set timer for 4 minutes. Start oven. *After each minute,* stir. Let stand 5 minutes. Makes about 1⅓ cups.

**1 tablespoon butter *or*
    margarine
2 tablespoons brown sugar
1 teaspoon cornstarch
1 8-ounce can crushed
    pineapple (juice pack)
⅛ teaspoon ground
    ginger**

● **Pineapple Topping:** Put the butter or margarine into a 4-cup liquid measuring cup. Do not cover. Place in the microwave oven; set on full or high (100%) power. Set the timer for 15 seconds. Start oven. If the butter is not melted after 15 seconds, micro-cook for 15 seconds more. Use a rubber scraper to stir in brown sugar and cornstarch. Use a can opener to open the can of pineapple. Add *undrained* pineapple and ginger to butter mixture. Stir till well mixed. Do not cover. Micro-cook on high 4 minutes, stirring *after each minute.* Let stand 5 minutes. Makes about 1¼ cups.

**1 6-ounce package (1 cup)
    semisweet chocolate
    pieces
¼ cup milk
1 cup tiny marshmallows**

● **Hot Fudge Topping:** Use kitchen scissors to open package of chocolate pieces. Put pieces and milk into a 4-cup liquid measuring cup. Do not cover. Place in the microwave oven; set on full or high (100%) power. Set the timer for 1 minute and 30 seconds. Start oven. After 1 minute and 30 seconds, if the pieces are not soft enough to stir smooth with a rubber scraper, micro-cook for 30 seconds more. Stir in the marshmallows. Micro-cook for 30 seconds more. Stir till smooth. Makes about 1¼ cups topping.

What's round, tastes like cake, and looks as if it were made just to hold a scoop of ice cream? It's a doughnut, the base for an unbeatable sundae treat. Top the doughnut with a scoop of your favorite ice cream, then pour on one of the warm toppings you've cooked in the microwave oven.

Make a peach melba sundae with peach ice cream and Raspberry Topping. Try a tropical sundae treat with coconut ice cream and Pineapple Topping. Pour the Hot Fudge Topping over chocolate or rocky road ice cream for a double-chocolate sundae. Or, create your own ice cream and topping combination.

To reheat any leftover topping after it has been chilled in the refrigerator, use a scraper to push the topping into a nonmetal bowl. Micro-cook, uncovered, on high for 30 seconds to 1 minute and 30 seconds. The reheating time will depend on how much topping is left over.

More than a Hint of Peppermint

EQUIPMENT

medium mixing bowl	measuring spoons
hot pads	2 plastic bags
wooden spoon	cutting board
measuring cups	meat mallet
	container

These doubly minty candies have peppermint extract on the inside, and crushed hard peppermint candies on the outside. The crushed candies give each piece a pretty, crunchy coating and extra flavor, too.

8 ounces vanilla-flavored confectioner's coating

● Put the confectioner's coating into a medium nonmetal mixing bowl. Do not cover. Place in the microwave oven; set on full or high (100%) power. Set the timer for 2 minutes. Start oven. After 2 minutes, use wooden spoon to stir. If not soft enough to stir smooth, micro-cook, uncovered, on high for 30 seconds more.

¼ cup whipping cream
⅛ teaspoon peppermint extract (about 10 drops)
Few drops red food coloring (if you like)

● Add cream, a little at a time, stirring hard after each addition till smooth. Add peppermint extract and food coloring, if you like; stir till mixture is evenly colored. Chill in the freezer for 20 to 30 minutes or till stiff enough to shape into balls, stirring *after every 10 minutes*.

7 to 8 hard peppermint candies

● Unwrap and crush candies, as shown. Use your hands to shape the chilled mixture into 1-inch balls, using about *2 teaspoons* for *each* ball. Roll each ball in the crushed peppermint candies, as shown. Chill at least 20 minutes before serving. Store in a covered container in the refrigerator. Makes about 20 candies.

Put the hard peppermint candies into a plastic bag inside another bag. Close bags. On a cutting board use a meat mallet to crush the candies, as shown.

Shape the mixture into balls, using about *2 teaspoons* for *each* ball. Then, roll the balls in the crushed peppermints till coated, as shown.

Microwave Heating Times for Dessert Foods

Is your sweet tooth nagging you for a bite of dessert? Why not heat your favorite topping and spoon it over ice cream? Or, try a warm slice of pie or gingerbread with a glass of milk. And, if you'd rather have something cold, you can make pudding or gelatin.

Gingerbread: Put one 3-inch square of *gingerbread* onto a small nonmetal plate. Micro-cook, uncovered, on high for 15 seconds. For 2 squares, micro-cook, uncovered, on high for 30 seconds.

Fruit Pie: Put one 4-ounce slice of *fruit pie* onto a small nonmetal plate. Micro-cook, uncovered, on high for 30 to 45 seconds or till hot. For 2 slices, micro-cook on high for 1 minute to 1 minute and 20 seconds or till hot.

Pudding: Use one package of 4-serving-size *regular pudding mix*. Measure *milk* into a 4-cup liquid measuring cup, following the package directions. Use a rubber scraper to stir in the pudding mix. Micro-cook, uncovered, on high for 5 to 6 minutes or till thickened and bubbly, stirring *after every 2 minutes.* Cover the top of the pudding with clear plastic wrap. (The wrap should touch the surface so a skin won't form.) Chill in the refrigerator for 1 hour. Spoon the pudding into dessert glasses and chill till serving time.

Ice Cream Topping: Put ½ cup of *ice cream topping* into a 1-cup liquid measuring cup. Micro-cook, uncovered, on high about 30 seconds or till topping is hot.

Flavored Gelatin: In a 4-cup liquid measuring cup combine one 3-ounce package of *flavored gelatin* and 1 cup of *warm water*. Micro-cook, uncovered, on high for 2 to 3 minutes or till hot. Use a rubber scraper to stir till the gelatin is dissolved (the liquid should be clear). Add *cold water,* following the directions on the package. Pour the gelatin into serving dishes and chill in the refrigerator about 2 hours or till gelatin is set.

For one 6-ounce package of *flavored gelatin,* combine gelatin and 2 cups of *warm water* in a 4-cup liquid measuring cup. Micro-cook, uncovered, on high for 3 to 4 minutes or till hot. Stir till gelatin is dissolved. Follow the directions above to finish making the gelatin.

Index

If you don't know where to start, look at this list of recipes. We've grouped them by how easy they are to make. If you've never cooked before, try making something from "For Beginners." When you feel comfortable with those recipes, move on to "For Advanced Beginners." Keep trying more and more recipes until you've tried those with the most steps (even they aren't hard). Then, you'll be a master chef.